ADVANCE PRAISE FOR

CLEVER

"CLEVER is more than an acronym or a framework. It sets the stage for a thinking paradigm to guide the reader towards the new tenets emerging from the Fourth Industrial Revolution, and inspire them with reflection and action on what needs to be done to thrive in this complex era. Written with wonderful fluidity, Alessandro's work is a new benchmark in the understanding of where society is heading and how it will evolve."

—Mark Esposito, PhD, Professor of Strategy, Hult International Business School and Harvard University, and co-author of the bestsellers, *The AI Republic: Building the Nexus Between Humans* and *Intelligent Automation &* DRIVE: *Understanding How the Future Unfolds*

"New technologies like AI, blockchain, and augmented reality are changing the rules of strategy and challenging established business models. From finance to healthcare, from oil and gas to manufacturing, from logistics to retail...no industry will be spared. Alessandro asks all the right questions to help business leaders navigate change and prepare for a very uncertain, yet very exciting future."

—Andrew White, PhD, Associate Dean for Executive Education and Corporate Relations, Saïd Business School, University of Oxford

"Rich in valuable examples and in thoughtful concepts, CLEVER is a book that will sit for a very long time on my desktop, as it should on yours."

—Hamoud Almahmoud, Editor in Chief, *Harvard Business Review Arabia*

"Alessandro's broad knowledge of business in a global world comes together as a thought-provoking framework to understand the future, which will be valuable to business leaders across industries."

—Andrea Galeotti, PhD, Professor of
Economics, London Business School

"CLEVER provides a logical and sound strategic framework to help people and organizations think strategically to decode, shape, and drive the challenges, opportunities, and complexity of the Fourth Industrial Revolution. What is remarkable about this book is the natural capacity of the author to produce a credible and pleasant narrative supported by academic rigour, captivating storytelling, and business acumen. The 'E' of CLEVER—Ethical Championship—is particularly compelling; the book offers dozens of 'hidden gems' unknown to most. A truly remarkable book we cannot afford to miss."

—Paolo Gallo, former Chief Human Resource Officer,
World Economic Forum, and author of
the bestseller, *The Compass and the Radar*

"Everyone talks about the Fourth Industrial Revolution and its transformational impact on every industry. CLEVER is your chance to understand its deep drivers and how to successfully respond to them. To that end, Alessandro Lanteri's recommendations are not only experience-driven and global, but—importantly—put ethics at the centre of value creation for the next frontier of our digital growth."

—Olaf Groth, Chief Executive Officer, Cambrian.ai
Berkley CA, and co-author of the bestseller, *Solomon's Code*

"The immense speed of disruptive change creates a huge challenge for business leaders to shape innovative organizations with agile teams and fast decision making. CLEVER provides a thoughtful framework for understanding the forces for change and helps create winning strategies for a successful future."

—Henning Schlutt, President,
Finance and IT, Alghanim Industries, Kuwait

"As international business becomes increasingly uncertain and the old rules of business become obsolete, business leaders need to explore new directions to stay successful. CLEVER provides a solid framework to understand the deep driver of change."

—Federico Donato, President of the Board of Governors,
European Chamber of Commerce in Singapore, and
council member, Singapore Business Federation

"The Fourth Industrial Revolution's unprecedented innovation speed is forcing companies to reconsider the frameworks that are tried and tested in many strategy books. CLEVER gives a fresh view to structure your thinking, and ought to be read."

—Xavier Rousseau, Head of Corporate Strategy, Snam SpA

"This book is hard to put down, both for what it teaches and for how it helps you think about the future."

—Andres Waldraff, Director of Innovation
& Analytics, Avianca, Colombia

"I particularly enjoyed the questions at the end of each chapter. Whenever I pick up the book and read one of them, it reminds me of why I was inspired to constantly rethink how we do things and why."

—Cris Knell, Executive General Manager,
Distribution, Suncorp NZ and board member of
Financial Services Council of New Zealand

"CLEVER kickstarts a deep conversation on the impact of new revolutionary technologies. It raises the right questions even when it may not have all the answers. Hard conclusions are a luxury one doesn't have in this fast-changing world of business, so everyone interested in the future of business should join this conversation."

—Denny Kurien, President and Chief Executive
Officer, Keiretsu Forum Delhi NCR and Bangalore

"Many business leaders see the symptoms of disruptive change but struggle to understand the forces that cause it. To chart a course to a successful future, you need to understand those fundamental forces in depth. CLEVER maps them out for you in very much detail, and helps you not only react to them, but seize the immense opportunities they offer."

—Konstantin Tsanis, PhD, Chief Innovation
and Data Officer, Wema Bank, Nigeria

"With the emergence of new digital technologies, value creation is constantly being redefined. CLEVER maps where to find the new drivers of value in the digital age."

—Andrea Di Camillo, Founder and
Managing Partner, P101 Venture Capital

"CLEVER sheds light on the strategic drivers behind some of the most innovative businesses shaping the global economy. A great read for anyone who wants to understand how a new breed of companies create value, now and in the future."

—Francesco Rattalino, PhD, Dean, ESCP Europe Turin Campus

"A compelling investigation of the transformative impact digital technologies have on organizations, business models, industries, and societies. It is hard to put down this book and harder still to stop thinking about the urgent challenges it raises."

—Mukul Kumar, PhD, Chief Innovation Officer,
Hult International Business School

"Conducting rigorous research on the future of business is notoriously hard. Ensuring the results of such investigation that business decision makers can immediately put to use is often beyond the realm of possibility. With CLEVER, Alessandro has masterfully achieved both."

—Terence Tse, PhD, Professor of Finance, ESCP
Europe, co-founder of Nexus Frontier Tech, and
co-author of the bestsellers, *The AI Republic: Building
the Nexus Between Humans* and *Intelligent Automation &
DRIVE: Understanding How the Future Unfolds*

"The CLEVER framework captures all the deep transformative forces that are redefining the competitive landscape, now and in the future, and provides invaluable guidance to managers and entrepreneurs alike."

—Nihel Chabrak, PhD, Chief Executive Officer,
UAE University Science and Innovation Park

"CLEVER was cleverly authored to help companies cope with exceptional change. The critical questions at the end of each chapter provoke thinking and deserve to be answered thoughtfully."

—Rassel Kassem, PhD, Head of Organizational
Development, Abu Dhabi Judicial Department

"Innovation used to give you an edge over your competitors. Now, everyone needs to innovate just to keep pace with the accelerating change. From startups to family businesses to corporations, CLEVER has a critical lesson for everyone seeking to innovate in this age dominated by change."

—Silvia Vianello, PhD, Director of Innovation, S P Jain
School of Global Management, and *Forbes* Top 100
Italian Women and Top Middle East Woman Leader

CLEVER

THE SIX STRATEGIC DRIVERS FOR THE FOURTH INDUSTRIAL REVOLUTION

ALESSANDRO LANTERI PhD

CLEVER

The Six Strategic Drivers for the Fourth Industrial Revolution

ISBN   978-1-5445-0652-4   *Paperback*

         978-1-5445-0651-7   *Ebook*

For my wife, Lera

CONTENTS

INTRODUCTION

I learnt how to drive at the age of three.

I had just learned how to write my name. So, my grandfather decided it was also time I learned how to drive.

A mechanic by profession, my grandfather made modifications to his own automobile. One such change was to the engine that allowed the car to drive without accelerating, even though it was a manual transmission. Placing the car in first gear let the car move on its own, albeit slowly. In that car, he taught me how to press the pedal to put it in gear. The car would move at a snail's pace, and I would sit in his lap and steer.

We never drove all that far together—only about ten kilometers to the next town and back. At the time—it was the early 80s—it would take just over one liter of fuel to make that journey.

With today's vehicles, one could make that drive using only half a liter. That means fuel efficiency has improved by nearly 45 percent in this period. This might seem like a noteworthy improvement. Yet, my grandfather was fond of repeating that there is no measurement without comparison. So, let's compare this improvement to another one that occurred during the same time frame.

In 1980, personal computers were slowly becoming affordable. At the time, internal hard drives were so expensive that most users employed external floppy disks instead. The state of the art was then the five-and-a-quarter-inch soft floppy, with a capacity of 160 kilobytes, capable of holding less than one second of high-quality music, which clocks in at 176 kilobytes.

Today, smartphones can store entire *weeks'* worth of CD-quality music. That represents an improvement in storage capacity of over *a million times*. The whole phone costs what the floppy reader would have, and it fits in your pocket. Combined, these improvements in storage capacity, size, and price demonstrate exponential improvement.

The improvement rate of fuel efficiency pales in this comparison. What if fuel efficiency had developed at that rate?

That brief drive from my childhood would barely utilize a drop of fuel. Gas stations would be a thing of the past— you would need only refuel perhaps once a year during your annual inspection. The cost of transportation would be drastically reduced. The expense of shipping goods would lower, which would then change the economics of manufacturing, because that manufacturing could take place in huge centralized factories to take advantage of economy of scale. That would increase the likelihood of workers moving to live closer to the factories, which would in turn change the demographics of the towns and cities.

In short, an exponential change in fuel efficiency comparable to that which occurred in digital technology would generate almost limitless ripple effects. The new technology would empower new business models, which would disrupt industries. This would transform the economy, and consequently lifestyles. Soon the world would look quite different than the one we now know. Of course, fuel efficiency is bound by the law of thermodynamics and so it cannot—and will not—evolve at such a rate.

Not so with digital technologies.

Digital technologies can grow at that exponential rate. Not only do they improve in efficiency, but they are continuously becoming smaller and more affordable. The hard drive in a current smartphone is incredibly small, and it is so affordable it is no longer sold separately, but simply included in the cost of the phone. In keeping with that evolution, data storage mounted on a device is quite quickly becoming obsolete, as cloud technologies continue to improve and mature.

Many technologies are changing—all at once, and by enormous factors. Artificial intelligence (AI), biotechnology, 3-D printing, robotics, nanotechnology, and driverless cars are only a few of the more commonly known examples. What is even more incredible is that as these technologies continue to improve, they work in tandem with each other to enhance the speed of their evolution. The end result is radically changing the world in which we live, and it is happening right before our eyes.

This is not a mere technological development. It's a revolution.

REVOLUTIONS HAVE CASUALTIES

We're at the beginning of a massive change that we don't yet entirely understand. This age of the Fourth Industrial Revolution—or 4IR—is one of ultra-rapid change, and it has consequences—both positive and negative.

As a leader, this pace requires you to make many more strategic decisions that are short-lived. According to the Boston Consulting Group, the average life of a business model was once fifteen years. By their estimation, that number has drastically reduced to *five* years.[1] Likewise, research by the bank Credit Suisse revealed that the average amount of time a company spends in the Fortune 500 has diminished from sixty years to *less than twenty*.[2] Such data suggests that even if you can rise to being one of the most successful companies in the world, it may not last.

The methods companies used to succeed in the past are no longer enough. In 2017, a number of business periodicals

---

1 "Business Model Innovation," Boston Consulting Group, accessed October 9, 2019, https://www.bcg.com/en-mideast/capabilities/strategy/business-model-innovation.aspx.

2 Michael Sheetz, "Technology Killing Off Corporate America: Average Life Span of Companies under 20 Years," CNBC, last modified August 24, 2017, https://www.cnbc.com/2017/08/24/technology-killing-off-corporations-average-lifespan-of-company-under-20-years.html.

began warning of a "retail apocalypse."[3] To some extent, they were correct. Companies that once netted immense profits have gone or are going out of business, or are being forced to pull back substantially. This includes enormous companies whose brands were household names, including Blockbuster, Kodak, Toys "R" Us and RadioShack.

These companies imploded because the world changed faster than they did. They couldn't evolve to keep pace with technological change and its effect on consumer habits. It's not just about poor management or bad decision making—those have always existed. The sheer number of companies closing their doors is indicative of the change brought about by the 4IR.

NEW CHALLENGES OPEN NEW OPPORTUNITIES

Revolutions also create entirely new opportunities. The 4IR is already witness to new start-up companies that are growing incredibly fast—on some occasions, going from zero to $1 billion valuations in only a few months. Facebook accumulated $1 billion in revenue in six years; Google, in only five. Instagram went from zero to a $1 billion valuation in fifteen *months*. From the moment I began working on this book until the time you held it in your hands, there were

---

3   Sinéad Baker, "The Retail Apocalypse Has Claimed 6,000 US Stores in 2019 so Far, More than the Number That Shut down in All of 2018," Business Insider, last modified April 17, 2019, https://www. businessinsider.com/retail-apocalypse-start-of-2019-more-store-closures-all-of-2018-2019-4.

surely a few companies that were created and are now worth several billion dollars.

This level of growth is not limited to the world of start-ups. Established companies are able to achieve this level of financial success as well—if they are able to learn and adapt.

But how? How do you become a success story and not a cautionary tale in this new landscape?

You must keep up with the speed of change. If you don't, you'll go the way of the dinosaurs of retail mentioned above. You have to make more strategic decisions, and you have to make them faster than ever before. The problem is that within this 4IR, the rules that you know for making strategic decisions are no longer enough. This is because the structure of the economy has changed. Managers need to look in new places for threats and find new sources for opportunities. In an age of rapid change, there is a price to pay for failure to notice how things are changing. Because this revolution is in its infancy, most people don't know where to look.

So, how do organizations succeed during the 4IR?

THIS BOOK

As a professor of entrepreneurship, executive educator, and advisor, I hear this question all the time. In the last year alone, I've worked with multinational companies, investors, consulting firms, international organizations, ministries, and other governmental organizations, start-up programs and, of course, educational institutions in a dozen countries on five continents. All want to know what they need to do for their organizations to remain successful in the face of this unprecedented change.

So, I set out to answer that question. The answer is this book.

Of course, the question of what makes organizations successful is not new and has been persuasively answered before. But we are now entering a new era. So, I needed to find new answers.

In my search for new answers, I examined the state of the art of academic research, which tends to lag behind the times, but has great theoretical rigor. I've analyzed reports by consulting companies, which tend to lack theory, but are rich in noteworthy cutting-edge case studies. Finally, I've engaged with people "in the field," to understand what stands in their way of making sense of the coming change, to make sure I addressed the genuine concerns of my readers.

In putting together my answer, I combined methodologies from business research and from the emerging discipline of future studies. I've examined over seventy case studies of multinationals, startups, and family businesses in multiple industries around the world. But case studies are mere *signals* of change. So, I dug deeper to uncover dozens of emerging trends. These are the *aggregated patterns* of change that describe many technologies, business models, and other similar signals. Yet, even these trends may be transient or declining. Therefore, I looked yet further to identify the *deep drivers* of these trends. Figure 1 clearly shows what these progressive levels of investigation mean.

The result is CLEVER, a research-based framework of strategic drivers, the handful of underlying forces that cut across companies, industries, geographies, and trends.[4]

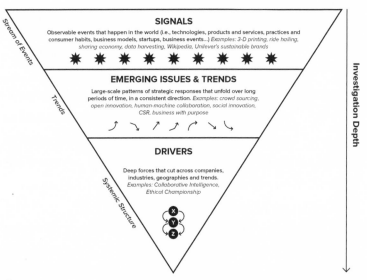

Figure 1.

Other books are exploring these phenomena, and most of them focus on one, or maybe two or three, of the drivers. Doing so makes it possible to discuss each in depth. There is an obvious trade-off between scope and depth. I find the drivers are not only interesting on their own, but they are especially interesting when you consider them together. If you look at them as a whole, you get a different perspective. That

---

4   UNDP Global Centre for Public Service Excellence. *Foresight Manual: Empowered Futures for the 2030 Agenda* (Singapore: 2018), 28, https://www.undp.org/content/dam/undp/library/capacity-development/English/Singapore%20Centre/UNDP_ForesightManual_2018.pdf.

is why I decided that they needed to be addressed not with a piecemeal approach, but as a comprehensive framework. CLEVER is a framework of six strategic drivers that help you navigate the 4IR. These are the deep forces that determine the viability of strategic decisions, now and tomorrow.

CLEVER

These six strategic drivers compose a comprehensive framework tailored to the challenges—and the opportunities—of the 4IR. The first three letters of the acronym represent the "hard" features—the technological components of the framework—while the second three capture decision-making and managerial styles.

C: COLLABORATIVE INTELLIGENCE

The organizations that best cope with the uncertainty of ultra-rapid change, do so by intelligently coordinating a broad range of skills. For example, they combine the skills of humans and machines and coordinate tasks that cater to their strengths. Another example is to tap into scattered crowds—using many human beings of diverse skillsets with different experiences, expertise, and origins, and coordinating them intelligently. Yet another example is open innovation—using knowledge and resources that are internal as well as external (e.g., consumer feedback, competitors, universities). The intelligent coordination of a broader range of skills allows outcomes that are not simply better, but otherwise altogether impossible.

L: LEARNING SYSTEMS

Today's organizations have access to incredible amounts of data. This information can provide unique insights into many sectors, but it's currently impossible for humans to parse such enormous data sets on their own. Organizations can use machine learning algorithms (or AI) to process these vast stores of data into a meaningful analysis to make decisions that are not only faster and more accurate, but also continuously become even faster and more accurate.

E: EXPONENTIAL TECHNOLOGIES

As in the mobile phone example, digital technologies are improving at an exponential rate. Moore's Law states computing power doubles every eighteen months, while halving in size and expense. If technology continues on this path at this speed, we will experience the equivalent of the last century's worth of innovation in the next twenty years. The threat of obsolescence is greater than ever. Organizations must recognize the early stages of exponential growth and make plans for how the world will be in one hundred years, relative to our current understanding of the future. They can then leverage that knowledge to take advantage of this massive disruption by supporting new industries and markets rather than letting it drive them out of business.

V: VALUE FACILITATION

In a market transaction, value is created by making an exchange with someone who values what you give them more than you do, in return for something that you value more than they do. However, the largest companies in the world no longer engage in transactions that create value this way. They create platforms that make it easier for *other people* to make these exchanges. Consider Airbnb. The value on that platform is created between the landlord and the tourist. Airbnb "merely" facilitates the exchange. Value Facilitation can be arranged almost entirely virtually in a way that allows companies that perform it to grow rapidly and exponentially. The larger the number of users on the platform, the greater the total value made possible. CLEVER organizations create platforms that facilitate these exchanges among users, and capture a portion of the value created from those exchanges.

E: ETHICAL CHAMPIONSHIP

The ethical standing of any economic actor is becoming increasingly critical because consumers assess it and reward it. We know from hard data that businesses that operate with a clear value proposition at their core—that do business with purpose—are often more successful for doing so. Economic actors are expected to have a positive impact on society and to have a positive role in it.

In addition, the largest unmet needs are those that are the most basic, and they are the needs of billions of the poorest people in the world in emerging economies. Serving them is not only a massively attractive business opportunity for organizations, but it also improves their lives. However, this effort must come from a place of true beneficence. Hollow, opportunistic efforts are easy to identify and can damage a company's reputation. Organizations that pursue a deeper purpose, sustain an ethical culture, and serve the unmet needs of large populations, become champions of value creation well beyond their financial bottom line.

R: RESPONSIVE DECISION MAKING

We live in a world that is changing rapidly, and as such, you must integrate Responsive Decision Making into your organizations. In the past, companies used to make five- or ten-year plans. While you need to have an idea as to what the future holds for your company, you can't have a rigid decision structure based on long-term planning. Instead of developing a fully realized product and launching it to market to see what works, you must instead develop a decision-making framework that is agile and responsive to the feedback you receive from the market. This becomes a discovery and learning process that allows you to be faster as an organization and significantly reduces the risk of poor decision making based on the rapid rate of change.

WHY THIS BOOK?

My work with clients and students centers on leadership and innovation—two terms with separate meanings, but that, in my view, are increasingly intertwined. Until recently, leadership was geared towards motivating individuals, in order to improve performance by increasing efficiency. Today, leading requires encouraging rapid learning and adaptation in order to facilitate changes—or innovation. So, there is a two-way connection between these concepts.

The organizations and business leaders that chose CLEVER to guide their strategic discussions keep repeating how valuable it has been for them. They tell me it helps them look for incoming threats and scout emerging opportunities in an entirely different way. They say it frames their thinking—that's what a framework should do. They feel less vulnerable to sudden disruption. This feeling helps them find the structure and the perspective to explore new paths to value creation. That's quite good—I do love it when my ideas help individuals and organizations become more successful—but not great.

As a professor, developing new knowledge and disseminating it in the most impactful way is both my job and personal mission. Educating a handful of brilliant MBAs and executives and helping a few organizations implement some parts of CLEVER is not enough. I needed to reach out to a broader audience. So, I set out to write this book.

USING CLEVER

This book is meant to encourage you to think strategically about your company and how you can best make decisions—or influence decision makers—to keep pace with ongoing change. It will help you know where to look when you're attempting to discern threats and when you're looking for direction and scouting opportunities. Successful leaders in the 4IR understand how the world around them is changing and make decisions to anticipate the change, respond to it, and make sure their company triumphs instead of disintegrating.

The first chapter explains the unique characteristics of the 4IR, and why it's urgent that companies prepare a plan of response. The next six chapters each explore one of the strategic drivers in detail. You'll see what each one encompasses, how it's being leveraged in the most successful case studies, and where it is headed in the future. Each chapter concludes with a set of questions you can use to understand how that driver applies to your business specifically.

The CLEVER framework is not a silver bullet—there is no quick fix here. It is an important tool that is only as good as the organization using it. You can pursue one driver, multiple drivers, or all of them. Whether you are an executive, a manager, or an entrepreneur, whether you work in a large corporation, a small one, or a family business, the last chapter tells you how to implement CLEVER in your business and how to align the rest of your company to follow your lead.

I won't promise that CLEVER will make you rich and successful, but I can tell you ignoring the drivers presented here will almost certainly lead to obsolescence. To prevent this, you need to better understand just what the Fourth Industrial Revolution is and how you can shape strategy to better navigate it.

However, this isn't just a book about strategy—it's a book about leadership. If you manage to do these things—understand the challenges of a fast-changing world, leverage CLEVER to design innovative solutions for your company, and successfully implement them—you've transcended from strategy into leadership. It is my sincere hope—both personally and professionally—that this book helps you become an extraordinary leader; that it gives you the tools to be more self-confident and to make better decisions; and that you bring about positive change through those decisions. That's what true leadership is.

—Alessandro Lanteri
London, Abu Dhabi, and countless
flights around the world
August 2019

CHAPTER ONE

THE FOURTH INDUSTRIAL REVOLUTION

ow do you create a new smartphone and sell it to millions of customers around the world *without investing in industrial scale*? What I mean is no factory, no employees, no trucks, no shops—no tangible capital.

You crowdsource the design of the phone to a scattered group of unknown professionals who self-coordinate and will get paid only if they succeed. You then outsource its manufacture and hire an express courier to deliver it right to the doors of your customers, wherever they might be on the planet. You can leverage your online presence or an existing online shop to reach these customers. None of this requires large investments in owning tangible capital.

If you attempted the same feat fifteen years ago? You would have to set up an enormous facility, install expensive machinery, prototype your phone several times, and test it to ensure it worked. Then, after all of that was complete, you would have to open shops around the world or strike deals with existing shops, then set up your logistics, and manage your warehouse. Then there is the training of thousands of employees to consider. It would be an impossible undertaking without significant amounts of upfront capital.

In their book *Unscaled*, venture capitalist Hermant Taneja and columnist Kevin Maney illustrate how the principles of mass production and economies of scale are being replaced by rentable industrial scale and mass customization.[1] Apple sells hundreds of millions of devices every year, but they don't manufacture (almost) any of them themselves. Instead, a company called Foxconn manufactures virtually everything Apple sells. Amazon has created a global retail empire without opening physical shops. With no need to invest in proprietary industrial scale, these companies easily increase their value by concentrating on providing the best products and services to the consumer.

---

1   Hemant Taneja and Kevin Maney, *Unscaled: How AI and a New Generation of Upstarts Are Creating the Economy of the Future* (New York: PublicAffairs, 2018).

The innovation expert Stian Westlake and the economist Johnathan Haskel illustrate how an "intangible economy" is rising and how capitalism no longer requires "capital."[2] Intangible assets change the rules of competition, because they have four unique properties: they can grow in value very quickly (i.e., they are *scalable*); they are not worth much in case of liquidation (they represent *sunk* costs); they can be easily copied and replicated (they are subject to *spillovers*); and they can only be protected through a mix of branding, design, marketing, and distribution (they require *synergies*).

In the past, we could create and capture significant value by doing physical work with tangible capital. We could create a large piece of machinery—a bus, for example—and sell it. Then, there would be a required system of maintenance to keep it running and effective. Tangible goods have not disappeared, to be sure. Yet, with globalization, low cost manufacturers are eliminating the profit margins from making them. Nonetheless, with digital technology, significant value is found not in creating new machines, but in making existing machines—like that same bus—more efficient. For example, we could engineer preventive maintenance so that the bus never has unplanned stops for repairs, or we could optimize its driving routes[3] to increase occupancy while consuming less fuel, making it a more efficient asset.

2   Jonathan Haskel and Stian Westlake, *Capitalism Without Capital: The Rise of the Intangible Economy* (Princeton, New Jersey: Princeton University Press, 2018).

3   Kara Baskin, "Creating Better Bus Routes with Algorithms," MIT Sloan School of Management, last modified July 31, 2017, https://mitsloan.mit.edu/ideas-made-to-matter/creating-better-bus-routes-algorithms.

The goal of all business activity is value creation—combining products and services such that they become more valuable together than they were apart. In an industrial revolution, the manner in which value is created fundamentally changes in response to substantial technological development. The previous methods of creating value rapidly become obsolete and new business models and organizations soon emerge. This shift drastically alters how our economy functions on every conceivable level. The businesses that actively respond to and embrace the new opportunities resulting from this change achieve success, while those that stick to the old ways tend to go out of business.

But what exactly is an industrial revolution?

THE FIRST THREE INDUSTRIAL REVOLUTIONS

When we discuss industry, we conjure images of large factories, chimneys billowing black smoke, where physical goods are assembled and then sold. While this still might be true in some cases, the examples above illustrate how times have changed. That does not mean that industrial revolutions do not occur.

An industrial revolution is a profound and irreversible transformation in the structure of the world economy.

The First Industrial Revolution occurred near the end of the eighteenth and into the beginning of the nineteenth century, triggered by the advent of steam power. The steam engine dramatically improved the efficiency with which products were created and the way people and cargo were moved from place to place.

It became far easier to mass produce goods, which meant that companies could create more standardized and refined products. Factories began to spring up. Bringing together people and large machines also created a new need: management positions. Before this, there was no need of management outside of the army and government. Because of technological advancement, the entire structure of businesses changed in a fundamental way.

At the end of the nineteenth century, another technological development reshaped the world economy. The utilization and widespread implementation of electricity drove the world's Second Industrial Revolution, also known as The Technological Revolution. Electricity dramatically increased the rate and scale of production, which led to the invention of the assembly line. Suddenly complex consumer goods could be produced much faster. This change also led to the creation of a new role—scientific managers who approached the flow of production in a scientific manner. They examined the most technically efficient means of manufacturing, as value was very much captured by physical output—the creation of products. Competition and strategy were geared toward having—and achieving—industrial scale.

In the 1950s, the invention of the transistor lay the groundwork for the creation of microprocessors and more powerful computers. This technological advance sparked the Third Industrial Revolution, also called The Digital

Revolution. Computers allowed for the automation of production and for dramatic improvements in communication technology, with the most significant example being the internet. We also began to realize that a great part of the value being created came from the sharing of knowledge and information. The ability to communicate information rapidly across the world and using digital technology to coordinate, facilitate, and increase efficiency was the driver for the conditions for our current global economy. A number of new roles arose from this shift, including project managers and strategic planners.

4IR

While we are still at the tail end of the Third Industrial Revolution, the conditions have already been created for the Fourth to emerge. This revolution was not sparked by radically new technological developments. Instead, the new technologies created during the Third Industrial Revolution are merging together to create an entirely new way for humans to interact with the world, knowledge, and even our own bodies.

Even in an age of unpredictable change such as 4IR, as we'll discuss later in the chapter, certain underlying forces consistently generate patterns of large-scale change that unfold over long periods of time and determine how economies and entire societies make decisions. In their book *Understanding How the Future Unfolds*, professors and authors Terence Tse and Mark Esposito call these patterns of change megatrends.[4] To gain some insight into the future, we need to understand these megatrends.

Three megatrends that emerged from the Third Industrial Revolution are especially critical to understanding this next revolution. The first is technology and innovation—the rise of digital computing and a lightning-fast internet.

This led to the second megatrend—globalization. Consider our earlier example of the creation of a new mobile phone. As we've said, in the past, the goal was to create physical goods and scale in order to make more of them, and more efficiently, because that was the source of value. However, with the increase in communication technology, one of the consequences is that we now live in a more globalized world. This means that different regions and geographies of the world can trade much more easily than ever before.

As a result, competition now comes from different countries. If you are Caterpillar or another established brand of heavy machinery, your competitors are now not only in America, but in Europe and China. In fact, according to the consulting company McKinsey[5] as much as 53 percent of the world's industrial machinery is now made in the Asia-Pacific

---

4   Terence C. M. Tse, PhD and Mark Esposito, PhD, *Understanding How the Future Unfolds: Using* DRIVE *to Harness the Power of Today's Megatrends* (Lioncrest Publishing, 2017).

5   Matthias Breunig and Niko Mohr, "Digital Machinery: How Companies Can Win the Changing Manufacturing Game," McKinseey Digital, accessed October 21, 2019, https://www.mckinsey.com/business-functions/mckinsey-digital/our-insights/digital-machinery-how-companies-can-win-the-changing-manufacturing-game.

region, up from just 28 percent in 1998. China and other Asian economies can make similar machinery for far less money, though often lower in quality. However, when customers can purchase three excavators from China for the price of one in America, they may take the trade-off in longevity of the product because three excavators will allow them to be far more productive in that time.

This competition from low-cost economies, made possible by globalization, is one of the main reasons why there is very little value anymore in the production of physical goods.

The third megatrend is a change in demographics because of increased mobility and consumption styles. These all contribute to the emergence of new models of creating value.

What follows are some of the major characteristics of the 4IR:

NEW TECHNOLOGIES

According to Professor Klaus Schwab, founder of the World Economic Forum and author of *The Fourth Industrial Revolution* and of *Shaping the Future of the Fourth Industrial Revolution*, the major technical developments in 4IR are a convergence of physical, digital, and biological technologies—and they are all evolving in parallel. [6] [7]

The Third Industrial Revolution brought the digital element into play. As such, the relationship between the digital

---

6   Klaus Schwab, *The Fourth Industrial Revolution* (New York: Crown Business, 2017).
7   Klaus Schwab, *Shaping the Future of the Fourth Industrial Revolution* (New York: Currency, 2018).

and the physical world is becoming something completely new and different. Cloud systems are more and more commonplace, and we now have the Internet of Things emerging and growing at a rapid rate. There are systems designed to collect massive amounts of data, exponentially increasing our knowledge base. We have new processors accelerating our computers, with machine learning and AI, allowing us to accumulate knowledge in ways we never could before.

CYBER-PHYSICAL SYSTEMS

When discussing how technological systems fuse with the digital world, Professor Schwab uses the term "cyber-physical systems." A cyber-physical system is a digital technology or computing system which has a direct effect, connection, and interaction with the physical world.

The digital developments take the shape of computer processors and algorithms that make it significantly easier to collect that data, analyze it, and make decisions. The physical developments have two components which are powered by new digital tech: physical sensors that let us gather data from the physical world and new technologies that affect the physical world, such as new materials, robots, and 3-D printing. Biotechnologies are the developments that affect biological life, including nanotechnology, the manipulation of particles on an incredibly small scale.

All three of these spheres of technology are evolving and accelerating change for each other and together. The more they change, the more they affect each other. Moreover, we can now draw information from the physical world, take that knowledge and make it digital, process it digitally, and learn more from it to create further change in the physical world. This means that the potential for change is exponential, as we will discuss in chapter 4.

EVOLVING SUPPLY AND DEMAND

According to Professor Schwab, these new technology-empowered cyber-physical systems are redesigning markets. When we analyse markets, we must look at both sides: the supply side and the demand side. What we see is that these new technologies are transforming the supply-side—the means of production and the ways companies can meet the needs of consumers. For example, it's now possible to 3-D print a spare part at a client's warehouse instead of manufacturing and transporting it. It makes the service faster, cheaper, and serves the customer better.

On the consumer side, we see that customers are substantially more engaged with what they do and what they choose. They have an expectation that their unique personal needs will be met, which means producers need to cater to more customized requests. In some instances, consumers become co-creators of value in platform systems like Airbnb and Uber. We will discuss how in chapter 5.

All of this rapid change has led to a landscape and environment that has become increasingly turbulent—and somewhat frightening to navigate. Identifying the factors that make it so can help to assuage some of those fears.

Let's take a closer look at the volatility, uncertainty, complexity, and ambiguity of this new world.

VUCA: VOLATILE, UNCERTAIN, COMPLEX, AND AMBIGUOUS

Not only are things changing faster than ever before, but they are changing in more dramatic ways, and it's difficult to discern where the next change is coming from.

That rate of change is volatility—the breakneck speed at which all of these technologies are evolving, at which they are becoming more widespread globally, and at which societies embrace them. This change is not only faster, but also more dramatic, and it affects business in new and unexpected ways.

Uncertainty means not knowing where change is coming from or what its effects will be. The only thing we can be certain of in today's VUCA environment is that there will be change. Not knowing where and how often leads senior managers to ignore change or assume that change will follow the same patterns as they're used to. Both are dangerous attitudes.

Complexity refers to the interconnectedness created by digital technology. The benefit of the globalization of communication also entails that changes reverberate globally, with unpredictable ripple effects that resemble complete chaos.

Finally, ambiguity refers to how difficult it is to see a clear cause-and-effect link between what happened and what will happen next. When it comes to new technologies, we don't know what long-term ramifications they hold. Consider the work of improving human DNA to defeat genetic cancers. Perhaps curing those diseases will lead to rapid overpopulation and eventual mass starvation. Or, perhaps this development will lead to decreased birth rates because once we know how long our offspring will live, we won't feel the need to have so many. Then again, neither of these could be true, and the advancement could lead to some other totally unforeseen result.

For a real-world example of these concepts, consider the financial crisis of 2008. It affected almost every country in the world—yet it began with a loan officer, in the branch of a bank somewhere in the US, that approved a loan for someone who truly couldn't afford it. That scenario was compounded by a number of other loan officers doing the same thing, and before long, we were in the midst of a financial crisis that stretched halfway around the globe, largely due to the interconnectedness—or complexity—of the global financial system. While likely every reader of this book was affected by that crisis in one way or another, very few of us, even in hindsight, are watching what today's loan officers in the US are doing. How can we? It's too much to keep track of. How many similar things might be happening all over the world?

The only thing to be done is to accept that radical change is coming. Because of the interconnectedness of today's business environment—because of its complexity, along with the other three elements of VUCA, we won't know where that change will come from, and whether or not it will be to our benefit or detriment. Regardless, we must accept and embrace this change. As we said in the introduction, change is not only a threat. It is also an incredible source of new opportunities.

But how do we prepare for a change that is unpredictable and out of our control?

We must become antifragile.

ANTIFRAGILE

In his book *Antifragile*,[8] Nassim Taleb discusses this concept. Imagine you have a box, and in that box, you place a number of delicate glasses which you plan to send via parcel as a gift to someone. Because you don't want the box to be handled too roughly—a metaphor for change and disruption—you place a "fragile" sticker on the outside. What if you filled that box with books instead? There would be no need for the warning sticker, because it wouldn't matter how people handled the box. No damage would occur because the books are robust, where the glasses are fragile.

As we enter an age of increasing disruption and change, it is important to ask ourselves: What we would put in the box such that we would place a sticker on the outside that reads "Handle roughly?" What would we put inside to encourage people to shake that box as much as they want, knowing that the more disorder and disruption we put those objects through, the stronger they will become?

Being robust is not enough. Something is only as robust as the disorder we can predict. If you can predict certain situations will occur, then it is possible to protect against those disruptions. However, what if the books that can be shaken caught on fire instead? What if they were dropped into a river? They would be destroyed. How do we create antifragility in the face of unknown disruptions?

---

8   Nassim Nicholas Taleb, *Antifragile: Things That Gain From Disorder* (New York: Random House, 2012).

One of my favourite examples is the Hydra, a terrifying mythical monster with multiple heads. The biggest disruption the creature can expect is when the hero arrives to save the day and lops off one of those heads. Any other monster would suffer defeat in such an instance—but not the Hydra. When the Hydra loses a head, two more grow in its place, making it stronger than before.

Why do people go to the gym? Why do they put their bodies through unnecessary stress, burning calories they don't need to burn, consuming energy they didn't need to consume, and sweating? Though the experience is unpleasant, their bodies react to that stress, becoming healthier and stronger.

Sometimes pursuing antifragility may seem unnecessarily painful or even counterintuitive.

For example, what can you do to ensure a stable career?

Change jobs every three years. Not the idea of stability you had in mind? By doing so, you put yourself through the stress, unpleasantness, and pressure of changing jobs, but simultaneously, you develop the ability to rapidly find new work and adapt to new professional contexts quickly. This way, when disorder hits—and it will—you will have already prepared to take advantage of it.

How do you ensure your company remains successful through rapid changes in your industry?

You should start making more mistakes. Again, not your idea of success? By constantly investing time and resources in trying new things—most of which will fail, because they are new and unknown—your company will learn what works. Let me reiterate: this way, when disorder hits—and it will—you will have already prepared to take advantage of it.

In this increasingly VUCA environment, is your business going to be fragile, like the disrupted companies you've seen before? You don't want that. Are you going to be robust so that you're indifferent and unaffected by the change? That's an illusion. You can only be resistant to the change you see coming. Lehman Brothers was as robust as could be, yet they never knew what hit them. How could they have been—how will you become—VUCA-proof?

Doing so requires the various new technologies and methodologies we will cover together in this book, and CLEVER is the framework that helps you think about how to move in this direction.

CHAPTER TWO

COLLABORATIVE INTELLIGENCE

Whenen Tesla launched its first mass market car, the Model 3, they used an extremely advanced automated assembly line to fulfill their orders.[1] The car was incredibly successful on the market and they experienced massive sales. They then encountered enormous problems because their automated

1   Alessandro Lanteri, "Tesla is Fixing its Automation Problems with...

facility couldn't manufacture the car fast enough to deliver it to their customers. The system encountered several problems that forced Tesla to stop and reengineer production on multiple occasions.

Other car manufacturers, like BMW and Mercedes, use automation and robots for certain stages of production like stamping, painting, and welding, all of which require accuracy and consistency. This is the work that machines are capable of doing better than humans.

However, in the final assembly stage, tens of thousands of parts and components have to be put together. At that point, assembling the car becomes a complex challenge— one that humans can handle quite well because they have the ability to solve those types of problems. Human beings have flexibility and the ability to improvise. Robots, as we know them today, are only able to keep doing the same tasks over and over again.

So, why did Tesla struggle?

Because it tried to have the robots do everything. A photo of the factory floor at Tesla showed no human beings. Tesla over-automated the process and tried to use robots to perform tasks better suited for actual people. In the end, Elon Musk, the CEO, resolved to bring people back to the process. Tesla then quickly got back on track with production.

In the aftermath, Musk quipped on Twitter that, "humans are underrated."

...Collaborative Intelligence," Hult International Business School, accessed October 21, 2019, https://www.hult.edu/blog/tesla-collaborative-intelligence/.

The bottom line is that the future of business isn't about replacing humans with robots. Yes, robots can increase productivity and reduce costs, but they can't perfectly replace human beings altogether. A more realistic goal is a Collaborative Intelligence where robots do the repetitive work that doesn't require the problem solving and innovation of which only human beings are currently capable.

HUMANS PLUS MACHINES

Machines are repetitive, predictable, and precise. They don't often make mistakes. Some people use this logic to suggest that since humans are more likely to make mistakes, it would be sensible to replace them entirely with machines in the workplace. Machines simply do not have the competence to replace all human jobs. With our current technology, we can only successfully replace about 5 percent[2] of human jobs and less than 50 percent of human tasks.[3]

Consider, for example, the different aspects of a professor's job. We prepare and give lectures, prepare and grade exams, give feedback, answer emails, and take attendance,

---

2   Michael Chui, James Manyika, and Mehdi Miremadi, "Where Machines Could Replace Humans—and Where They Can't (Yet)," McKinsey Digital, accessed October 21, 2019, https://www.mckinsey.com/business-functions/mckinsey-digital/our-insights/where-machines-could-replace-humans-and-where-they-cant-yet.

3   Carl Benedikt Frey and Michael Osborne, "The Future of Employment: How Susceptible are Jobs to Computerisation?" Oxford Martin Programme on Technology and Employment, September 17, 2013, https://www.oxfordmartin.ox.ac.uk/downloads/academic/future-of-employment.pdf.

among other things. Perhaps 30 percent of those tasks can be automated and performed at a high-quality level without supervision: taking attendance, grading exams, answering fairly simple questions, etc. The rest are still too complex for machines to master. What will most likely happen is that going forward, my job will no longer be completed by me alone—it will be performed by a team, and that team would be me and a machine. There are conceptual challenges that would need to be overcome, including how I as a professor would coordinate and collaborate with a machine, but the expected output would be that the two of us would perform the job better than either of us could do separately.

At its core, the question of Collaborative Intelligence is how to combine human capabilities with technological capabilities in the most effective way rather than simply replacing one with the other. In the next chapter we will discuss the types of tasks for which machines are especially well-suited. In the context of this discussion, it is also important to point out that there is a third level of task—those that are entirely new to both humans and machines.

Paul Daugherty and Jim Wilson, of the consulting company Accenture, address these three skillsets in their book *Human + Machine*. There is a set of skills where humans acquire superpowers by working with machines, and other skills where machines become super powered by collaborating with humans.

Humans train, explain, and sustain. In other words, they teach machines what to do and how to do it. They also have to understand how and why machines make certain decisions and finally analyze that information so that they can fix the machines and improve their processes over time to correct for change according to human values.

What the machines allow humans to do is to amplify, interact, and embody. Amplification means that machines have the ability to provide humans with real-time data processed in a way that allows people to make much better decisions than they would without it. The concept of interaction is that machines let you command, control, and communicate with machines in a more intuitive manner, using things like voice control. Technology such as Siri and Cortana are examples. Embodiment can be exemplified by robot-surgery. A physician can control a mechanical arm to execute an exceedingly precise and difficult surgery that would be next to impossible to perform unassisted by the technology.

I (AND) ROBOT

When talking about machines, I refer to any automatic system largely powered by AI. I cover this in detail in chapter 3. A specific type of machine, which naturally comes to mind as collaborators are robots.

People have an image from the movies and pop culture of robots as futuristic androids or humanoids capable of human emotions and other incredible abilities, but robots don't generally look like that. In popular culture, we refer to many items as robots that don't qualify as such. A robot is a physical machine capable of complex autonomous behavior. A driverless car, for example, is a robot; it's a physical piece of machinery that can make sophisticated and complex decisions by itself. A drone, on the other hand, is not a robot because it is controlled remotely by a human. In finance, a robo-advisor that makes investment decisions is not a robot. Yes, it can make complex decisions, but it has no physical component.

The truth is, we currently live with robots all around us. Roomba, the robot vacuum cleaner, makes complex navigational decisions on its own. A robotic arm in the Tesla factory works alongside humans to build cars.

THE FOUR Ds

Due to their quality of excelling at a single task and their lack of sentiments, we most commonly use robots to execute the "Four D" tasks: those that are dull, dirty, dangerous, and dear.

- *Dull:* Tasks that are extremely repetitive in nature. They are boring, predictable, and easy for machines to learn. Often these jobs are manufacturing-related, such as screwing on bottle caps.
- *Dirty:* Tasks that are unpleasant for humans, such as mining and cleaning sewers.
- *Dangerous:* Tasks where a human's physical health or survival would be at stake, such as space exploration, identifying land mines, and defusing bombs. You often see these types of robots in war zones.

- *Dear:* Tasks that are expensive for humans to perform. Using a robot increases efficiency and reduces costs.

It is great news that humans do not have to perform such tasks.

HUMANS PLUS HUMANS

The core notion of Collaborative Intelligence—to combine different skillsets so that they jointly achieve what they can't achieve separately—is not limited to humans collaborating with machines. Humans have broad ranges of skillsets that can be fruitfully combined to achieve improved performance.

James Surowiecki popularized this notion in his book *The Wisdom of Crowds*, where he shows how large groups, where individuals involved don't know one another and are scattered outside of an organization, can come together to solve a challenge or answer a question.[4] There are specific characteristics that make crowds useful. Within an effective crowd, you will find a diverse group of people with different skills and experiences. They do not have a strict hierarchy and are able to self-organize as necessary.

Even within companies, professionals from different functions, divisions, and cultures are increasingly brought to work together in temporary, cross-functional teams capable

---

4   James Surowiecki, *The Wisdom of Crowds* (New York: Anchor Books, 2005).

of rapidly solving very complex problems by leveraging their different skills. In their book *Collaborative Intelligence,* Dawna Markova and Angie McArthur explain in detail how to develop and manage the ability to "mind-share."[5]

Sadly, the smartest and most talented people cannot all work for your company. Most of them work elsewhere. Yet, this does not necessarily mean that you need to give up on their talent. The companies that dominate 4IR embrace open innovation. According to Professor Henry Chesbrough, this is a more distributed and participatory approach to innovation, where companies use external as well as internal ideas.[6] In other words, organizations too can collaborate intelligently with other organizations.

As discussed in the introduction, all these are crucial trends. Yet, there is more to them. They are all responses to a deeper driver: Collaborative Intelligence.

GREATER THAN THE SUM OF ITS PARTS

Combining intelligence doesn't simply reflect the individual characteristics of those in a group, but other emergent properties as well.

The notion of "emergent properties" refers to the characteristics unique to aggregate systems. For example, water

5   Dawna Markova, PhD and Angie McArthur, *Collaborative Intelligence: Thinking with People Who Think Differently* (New York: Spiegel & Grau, 2015).

6   Henry Chesbrough, *Open Innovation: The New Imperative for Creating and Profiting from Technology* (Boston: Harvard Business School Publishing Corporation, 2006).

is made up of hydrogen and oxygen, but understanding all the properties of the elements hydrogen and oxygen won't help you to fully understand the properties of water. When two hydrogen atoms and one oxygen atom are combined, they become something else entirely. In the same way, the human body is made up of more than 60 percent water, but we can't use the properties of water to predict 60 percent of what humans' bodies do.

Emergent properties aren't simply the characteristics that individuals bring to the table—they develop collectively, as well. You can take several talented soccer players and put them together on a team, yet you won't necessarily have a team that consistently wins. The manner in which the group works together depends on a number of complex factors.

Professor Thomas Malone[7] and his team at MIT conducted research on team performance and Collaborative Intelligence. They found that teams that displayed group intelligence showed high levels of social sensitivity, or emotional intelligence. This research points to groups becoming more intelligent when they work collaboratively. It is important to note that this has nothing to do with IQ or individual expertise—these teams were respectful of one another and allowed people to take turns communicating and contributing. The positive group dynamics made it easier for different skills to combine and contribute to a joint outcome.

---

7   Anita Woolley and Thomas W. Malone, "Defend Your Research: What Makes a Tear Smarter? More Women," *Harvard Business Review* (June 2011).

As we discussed in the last chapter, our 4IR world is increasingly VUCA: volatile, uncertain, complex, and ambiguous. Individuals don't possess the awareness, knowledge, expertise, and skills to make sense of a VUCA world on their own. However, combining multiple skillsets from different people and machines make it much easier for us to perceive, understand, and make decisions in a complex world.

How do all these concepts of Collaborative Intelligence come together in practice?

THE POWER OF THE CROWD

Consider the story of Jimmy Wales and Larry Sanger, the founders of what ultimately became Wikipedia. They started a project aiming to create an online encyclopedia in the late 1990s, when online forums were still a new and exciting technology. They saw that people were willing to contribute their knowledge online for the common good, so they used an online forum approach to create what they called Nupedia.

The idea was multi-faceted. First, they wanted to find experts with PhDs in their fields, assign them entries to write, have other experts review the content, then solicit professional editors to polish the articles. After that portion of the process was complete, the content was submitted to an administrator for final approval. The methodology was structured, rigorous, and linear, but early results were lacking. Only twelve entries were completed over the course of a year, at a cost of more than $250,000 in production and labor. With so much money spent and so little to show for it, the project looked to be doomed.

Then, in the early 2000s, a new wave of sites called wikis began appearing on the internet. People could post information, or just their thoughts, as on a bulletin board. In a desperate attempt to save their project, Wales and Sanger created the wiki called Wikipedia. They did not seem to have high expectations when they invited participants on the wiki. In an email, Sanger wrote:[8] "Humor me. Go there and add a little article. It will take all of five or ten minutes."

Within a few months, a community of random internet contributors with no specific credentials and from a variety of backgrounds contributed whatever information they knew on a wide range of topics. Some even donated their editing and review skills. What they created is now the largest general reference site on the internet.

Wikipedia became one of the greatest examples of how crowds create value and redefine entire industries. Prior to its development, whatever was found in print encyclopedias was generally a decade old because it took years to produce and edit a volume. That system was doomed to eventual obsolescence. In a less VUCA age, physical reference volumes worked. However, next to no one would buy a print encyclopedia with all of the current technology available to find that same information. Thanks to the rapid pace at which our world moves, information from an expert even five years ago is inadequate and outdated in most fields of knowledge.

---

8 Clay Shirky, "Wikipedia—an Unplanned Miracle," *The Guardian*, last modified January 14, 2011, https://www.theguardian.com/ commentisfree/2011/jan/14/wikipedia-unplanned-miracle-10-years.

Wikipedia is an example of the power of the crowd. It also shows the power of combining crowds with computers into hybrid systems.

HYBRID SYSTEMS

Wikipedia also makes use of a hybrid system to refine its product. It employs bots to perform critical work that is quite time consuming for humans, such as verifying that content is not plagiarized. Doing this by hand would take decades, but for an algorithm, it is a fairly simple task to complete. A bot can compare what percentage of a text is like another text and flag it instantaneously, if necessary. Then, a human being can step in to make an informed decision. The combination of the crowd and the bots—a Collaborative Intelligence—reimagined the encyclopedia as we know it and created new value.

There are many more examples of how crowds, humans, and computers collaboratively generate increasingly intelligent, hybrid systems.[9]

Take, for example, a famous chess match in the late 1990s that pitched the Russian chess champion, Gary Kasparov, versus a crowd of 50,000 chess players around the world who connected via the internet and voted on which moves to make. Kasparov won, but he found the experience so profound that he later wrote a book dedicated to that single

---

9   Andrew McAfee, "Did Gary Kasparov Stumble Into a New Business Process Model?" Harvard Business Review, last modified February 18, 2010, https://hbr.org/2010/02/like-a-lot-of-people.

game of chess. He was quoted as saying, "the sheer number of ideas, the complexity, and the contribution it has made to chess make it the most important game ever played."[10]

Kasparov was later to play yet another "most important game ever," the one against an IBM computer known as Deep Blue. The crowd could not defeat the champion, but he wanted to test himself to see if a computer could. This was largely due to the fact that Kasparov knew that chess could be played in two distinct ways—as a creative endeavor, or as a rote computational power task. Computers play chess by surveying the board and then calculating an incredible number of contingencies and possible evolutions and developments of the game. For each of their moves, they calculate a statistical probability of winning. They continue those calculations until time runs out, and when it does, the computer makes the move that gives it the highest likelihood of winning. In this way, a machine can potentially out strategize a human.

Kasparov won the first match in 1996. Just one year later, Deep Blue had improved enough to defeat the human champion.

In an article years later,[11] Kasparov described a game where two solid but average chess players—not master players like himself—with a decent laptop played in a tournament and won against master chess players and super computers. They accomplished this by letting their quite average laptop make calculations that offered them a selection of move

10 Tim Harding, *64 Great Chess Games* (Dublin: Chess Mail Ltd., 2002).
11 Garry Kasparov, "The Chess Master and the Computer," *The New York Review of Books* (February 11, 2010).

options based on massive data crunching that would have been impossible for them to complete without a machine's help. The two players looked at that data, coordinated on the most promising move on the board and, depending on who they were playing against, executed that move. The humans contributed executive decision making and intuition. The machine handled the data analysis. Together they defeated everyone put in front of them.

This is the core of Collaborative Intelligence—a combination that together creates an outcome that would otherwise be unimaginable, even by superior entities or experts.

How then do we transfer this to the business world?

BUSINESS APPLICATIONS FOR COLLABORATIVE INTELLIGENCE

We know now that humans need to be assigned to tasks that require executive decision making, creative problem solving, and creativity. Machines should be assigned to activities that require consistency and predictability.

In between those poles are a set of tasks—the "missing middle"—that function best with a combination of human and machine work. The magic here happens when humans contribute their unique skills to machines, and machines give their unique skills to humans. In the Wikipedia example above, humans contributed their ingenuity and expertise, while machines contributed in the form of bots and algorithms that made complicated tasks simple.

This symbiotic relationship between humans and machines gives rise to what we called "hybrid skills." The emergence and proliferation of hybrid skills means that soon work will no longer be performed by individual humans, but in small teams of humans and robots. Our future coworkers will likely not be human, so the potential for human error will be diminished greatly. Yet, in his book *Superminds*, Professor Malone notes that not everything humans do will eventually be replaced by machines.[12] Rather, an increasing number of tasks we perform will be *improved* by machines.

This application of Collaborative Intelligence might drastically change the way we look at work and what it means to contribute. Technology can be used as a tool we manipulate—someone can make rules for a spreadsheet, press a button, and the computer does exactly what it is told. There is nothing new here. It's effectively the same concept as using a farming tool or an abacus. Humans remain fully in charge.

Yet, increasingly, technology can also act as an assistant or peer. As an assistant, it helps humans perform their tasks. As a peer, it does the work of an employee, with a human only intervening to solve more difficult issues.

For example, imagine a traditional delivery warehouse. In it, a human would have a station, roam around the warehouse to collect items to fulfill an order, and then return to the station to assemble the package. Then, someone else would check the box to make sure the contents are accurate and load it into a delivery vehicle. Compare that process to that of an Amazon warehouse. There they have a fleet

---

12 Thomas W. Malone, *Superminds: The Surprising Power of People and Computers Thinking Together* (New York: Little, Brown and Company, 2018).

of robots called KIVA that roam the warehouse. When they identify the correct shelf on which the item is located, they drive that shelf to a human. The human then easily picks and packs the correct item. In this process, the human never has to leave their station. The KIVA robots are assistants.

Additionally, instead of a human inspecting every single package, a machine weighs each box. If the weight is correct, the package can be shipped. If there is a weight discrepancy, the system flags the mistaken package. Here, the weighting system does the same job as a human did. It's a peer. Humans only step in to handle the more complex situations. When a package is the wrong weight, they open it and troubleshoot.

The difference in workflow at a traditional warehouse versus Amazon's warehouse shows how we can transform the relationship between humans and machines, all the while increasing efficiency. The robot does the tedious searching and the heavy lifting, while the human does the more specific packing of items. All tasks are performed by hybrid teams of humans and machines.

What is the relationship between humans and machines in this collaboration?

MACHINES AS MANAGERS

As just seen, machines are no longer mere tools in our hands. They are increasingly assistants that help us perform our tasks more effectively and even peers that can altogether replace us in some tasks. There is a fourth role—an additional relationship between humans and machines—and that is where the machine decides, and the human obeys. The simplest example is that of a traffic light. The machine turns the light red, and you know you have to stop.

Of course, this is now becoming much more advanced. When an automated system tells you what the right decision is to make, that begins to redefine the relationship between man and machine.

Furthermore, it affects our understanding of what it means to be good at our jobs—to be a professional or an expert. This presents a major obstacle that you as a decision maker will have to face as you move into the 4IR because you will still have to coordinate and motivate human beings. When you put a human being in a team with a machine that tells the human to do something he doesn't understand, the dynamics of that team will have to be managed.

We don't know how to do that yet. There is no notion of leadership or team management that tells how to coordinate the human and the machine. I consider this the greatest leadership challenge moving forward.

THE FUTURE OF COLLABORATIVE INTELLIGENCE

Collaborative Intelligence is not exclusively a human affair. The natural world is rich with examples we can learn from. For instance, an individual honeybee has very narrow intellectual capabilities, limitations on how far it can fly, and restrictions on what it can perceive and interpret. However, combine six hundred bees together, and their intelligence and capabilities increase. As a hive, they manage to coordinate and communicate to handle huge decisions, such as leaving one location and establishing a new hive elsewhere.

When selecting a location for a new colony, honeybees face a life-or-death decision. Research by Tomas Seeley at Cornell University explains how bees often choose the best available spot for the new hive.[13] After searching a thirty-square-mile area, scout bees bring information about dozens of potential sites back to the swarm for consideration. Each site is evaluated for factors that include safety from predators, insulation for winter, ventilation for summer, and storage capacity for honey. Using body vibrations, the scout bees form a real-time swarm where they express preferences for various sites based on those factors. Through negotiation among the signals, the hive reaches a decision—and they make the optimal decision *80 percent of the time.*

There is no indecision. No opinion is given more weight than another. Even though individual bees are quite unintelligent by any standard definition, a hive of bees share individually collected information and aggregates it into something far greater than the sum of its parts. Humans aren't quite as skilled as that yet, but there are many new techniques and methods to organize people's individual skills into a sort of "hive mind."

A system called UNU recruited people without any previous experience picking Oscar winners and asked them to

---

13 Carl Zimmer, "The Secret Life of Bees," *Smithsonian Magazine* (March 2012).

predict the winners of the Academy Awards. The system pitted this group of novices against a panel of movie experts. The non-competent individuals voted together as a group and chose six out of fifteen Oscar winners correctly. The group of movie experts chose nine out of fifteen picks correctly, meaning they were better at this task as a collective. UNU then employed the "swarm approach," where instead of everyone simply voting, they had the chance to persuade each other of their reasoning for making each Oscar pick. With the swarm approach, the non-competent group outperformed the experts by correctly picking eleven of the fifteen Oscar selections.

Some believe that AI will eventually boost humanity to a stage where we will be able to make decisions not individually, but as if we were one collective body or hive. There is also the idea that people are moving toward a singularity where all minds are connected and coordinated by some artificial intelligence. We would all contribute our own intelligence and skills, making it possible for us to achieve things humans would never individually achieve, even with the use of machines.

This is a heady concept, and even a bit frightening for some to consider. We can't know for sure when (or if) this next step in Collaborative Intelligence will occur. Yet, the more uncertain and ambiguous our ecosystem, the more our success depends on intelligent collaborations with individuals and machines that have a broad range of different skills.

QUESTIONS

1. How often do you look beyond your internal experts for a solution to an existing problem?
2. When was the last time your company collaborated with a competitor to solve a common problem?
3. Where does your company engage with the crowd?
4. What tasks in your workplace are repetitive, predictable, boring, or dangerous?
5. What new products or services could you create by combining the reliability of machines with human skills?
6. How frequently do people work alongside colleagues from different departments?

CHAPTER THREE

LEARNING SYSTEMS

have a godson named Giovanni. When he was a year and a half old, I remember spending a whole afternoon with him. He would point at random places or things and utter one of two simple words—"Ma" or "Mu." To be honest, initially it sounded quite strange to me.

However, as I spent more time with him, I realized there was a logic to it.

Whenever Giovanni pointed at an animal, whether that animal was a toy, a print on his T-shirt, or a poster; whether it was a rooster, a horse, a cow, or a sheep; no matter what the animal, he called it "Ma." If he saw any vehicle, be it a toy airplane or a real boat, he called it "Mu."

I found it fascinating that he had this concept that all the animals had something in common—regardless of whether they were real animals, photos, or toys. Even though he was unable to speak beyond those two vocalizations, he identified that they had the commonality of being animals. The same held true for vehicles.

For a child, doing this is apparently quite easy, even before he can speak intelligibly. However, training AI to do the same is at present an impossibly hard task. Using the example of my godson and the animals, you would have to list an exceedingly large number of features that all of the animals have in common, irrespective of whether they are print, stuffed toys, or real animals. To explicitly list all of the features that all animals have in common—features that would allow a child to identify and differentiate them as "Ma" or "Mu"—would be an impossible task for a human, and therefore would be impossible to give those instructions to a computer.

One reason for this is that we are simply not aware of what these features are. It would take us years to list all the features that make us aware of what a real boat, a toy airplane, and a motorbike printed on a T-shirt have in common. Even in 2019 there is no AI, to my knowledge, that can do the things my then eighteen-month-old godson could do without any training whatsoever.

In some ways, it's quite counterintuitive. We talk about AI in an almost fearful way, intimidated by the incredible feats it can and supposedly will accomplish, yet it is still unable to match the capabilities of a child who can't yet speak.

ARTIFICIAL VERSUS HUMAN INTELLIGENCE

When we speak about AI, we speak about algorithms, or automatic systems that make decisions or perform actions.[1] These algorithms use data as input and process it to generate outputs that *appear* to be intelligent by human standards. Note that the critical word there is *appear*.

Let's see what they look like.

Nowadays, Google is one of the recognized kings of AI. One of their most popular services, Google Translate, allows you to type almost anything into their site and Google will recognize the language you are using and provide a translation into virtually any other language. Considering the speed at which this machine can translate, the intelligence of the system is apparent. Yet, is it genuinely intelligent?

There are two ways to create a technology with capabilities as robust as those of Google Translate. One is to sit down and have humans painstakingly code all possible translations into all possible languages. This task would take thousands, perhaps millions, of years. That is to say that it's beyond the reach of any human being or organization. The second, and significantly more efficient way, is to program a computer system to learn how to translate by itself.

---

1   Jerry Kaplan, *Artificial Intelligence: What Everyone Needs to Know* (New York: Oxford University Press, 2016).

This idea—that the system can learn and improve on its own, what is called Machine Learning—is the core of AI as we conceptualize it today.

WHAT ARE LEARNING SYSTEMS?

Algorithms can autonomously identify the common traits of certain entities and recognize that all of the manifestations of these entities have the same traits or features in common.

Said another way: if you train an algorithm to recognize dogs, the algorithm identifies all of the characteristics that are typical of dogs and they determine what these characteristics are, even though the humans are not aware of them. Once they have been identified, these traits become an algorithm, which means that every time you show the algorithm input such as a photo of a dog, the algorithm will generate the output of a tag that says, "This is a dog." It creates a statistical correlation between the features that we coded for.

The same thing occurs in all of the applications of AI, from language translation to recognition of voice commands. It associates a certain input and its characteristics to a certain output or tag—in this case, a dog. For a child of eighteen months, this is innate—it is a natural ability that they develop and that expands rapidly to include such detail that it would be impossible—at least currently—for a computer to emulate.

These algorithms are examples of narrow AI because they have learned how to perform a single task. An algorithm can learn to translate a French sentence into Chinese or Swahili, but it cannot understand the very same sentence if it is spoken. That requires an entirely different algorithm. Neither algorithm has any understanding of what it means to be French or Chinese. They don't comprehend the content of the sentence it translated. For example, if the sentence is about the smell of a madeleine cookie, AI has no concept of what a smell is or what a madeleine is. It certainly cannot draw on childhood memories triggered by the smell. In fact, it doesn't know what a memory or a childhood is.

Such a complex mesh of associated meanings and the ability to connect written and spoken words with elements of the broader culture are essential components of human intelligence. While Google Translate *appears* intelligent, it's not—at least not in any meaningful way. This is why I don't like to talk about Artificial Intelligence, and I prefer Learning Systems.

How do these systems learn?

LEARNING LIKE A MACHINE

There are three major approaches to Learning Systems: supervised learning, unsupervised learning, and reinforcement learning. Figure 2 represents them.

SUPERVISED LEARNING

Supervised learning involves showing an algorithm hundreds of thousands of examples of something accompanied by a human-generated description. For example, we could show an algorithm thousands of images of a dog and tag each with the word "dog." Eventually, the machine learns that certain combinations of characteristics in those images are statistically associated with the word "dog." Now, when we show that same machine a new photo of a dog, it can identify the animal correctly because certain attributes of the picture lead it to believe that it is probably a dog.

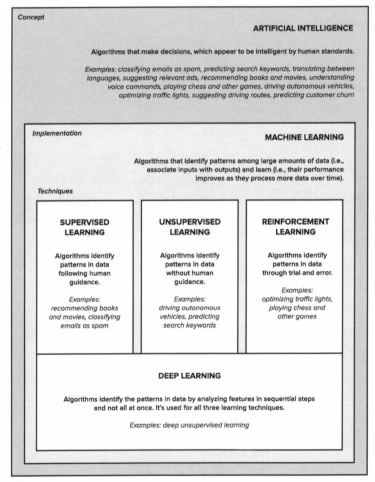

Figure 2.

Remember: the machine doesn't have any idea what a dog is. There are photos online of blueberry muffins that look remarkably like puppies, with the blueberries carefully positioned in a similar pattern to that of a dog's nose and eyes. A human can see the similarity but has no problem immediately telling the difference between a dog and a muffin. Yet, for a computer, this is a very difficult task. They can easily confuse muffins[2] and puppies if they look similar enough. If a system were to completely dispense of humans and only use this type of intelligence, you might find it serving you a puppy for breakfast by accident!

Again, these systems have no actual intelligence in a conventional sense. They are talented at learning statistical correlations between data. The more data they have, the better they can make decisions. This same supervised learning is how Gmail distinguishes between spam and desired emails. The algorithm has learned over millions of examples that emails with certain content or coming from certain senders are systematically flagged as spam or moved to trash without being opened. Hence, undesired emails no longer pop up in your inbox, but are automatically sent to the trash. Unfortunately, because these systems do not understand actual meaning, an important email may occasionally end up in spam. However, as these systems are fed more and more examples, they become increasingly accurate. This is authentic learning.

---

2   James Cave, "Is This a Muffin or a Chihuahua?: Too Hungry to Tell." HuffPost, last modified March 10, 2016, https://www.huffpost.com/entry/muffin-or-chihuahua_n_56e05c3ee4b065e2e3d461f2.

UNSUPERVISED LEARNING

In unsupervised learning, no tag is provided to the algorithm. You only feed it large amounts of data. The system then processes that data on its own and identifies patterns within it where even humans cannot. It's a technique often used in marketing because it is possible to take spending habits, preferences, and other behaviors and give them to the algorithm. The algorithm then creates a cluster of consumers who have certain characteristics in common that would have been unidentifiable by a human. Humans focus on demographics and income because those are the most obvious data sets—but they are not necessarily the most relevant to marketing efforts. Unsupervised learning, in this case, solves for that problem.

Autonomous vehicles can also learn. Again, there are two ways to train their Learning Systems. One method is to give them detailed instructions about what to do in the presence of certain situations—if there is an object within ten meters, then brake. Listing in detail all of the possible contingencies that are necessary in order for this vehicle to drive safely would, again, take thousands of years and it is a task we as humans are unable to accomplish.

However, we can give the algorithm all of the data points about the behavior of human driving. Instead of understanding and learning the rules of driving, the systems become quite good at predicting what a human would do in a given circumstance. We don't have to tell them what to do or why—we only show them how it's done. Then they figure out their own rules. In other words, autonomous vehicles and the systems that regulate them are being developed by showing them extraordinarily large amounts of examples that allow them to best replicate the same behaviors according to their own understanding of the scenarios.

REINFORCEMENT LEARNING

A variant of unsupervised learning is reinforcement learning. It means that you specify the rules of the game and a standard of successful performance, and then let the algorithm learn on its own how to succeed, by trial and error. A very famous example of this is AlphaGo, developed by Google's DeepMind to master the ancient game of Go, a strategy game vastly more complex than chess. AlphaGo played millions of games against itself, until it learnt the best strategy to win each game. Nobody had taught it how to do so.

The result? In 2016 it defeated Lee Sedol, the world champion at the time and widely considered one of the most talented human players ever. In 2017, a new version of the algorithm, AlphaZero, trained itself to a superhuman level of playing in just twenty-four hours. It also learnt how to defeat any opponent in chess and shogi (Japanese chess).

The power of this technique is that it is independent from the large amounts of data required to train other algorithms. Consequently, it also needs less computational power. This approach to Machine Learning is fast growing, but it is still secondary relative to supervised and unsupervised learning.

While applications of reinforcement learning to complex games capture the headlines, it is now being deployed to less mundane tasks, such as controlling robots, optimizing traffic lights systems to minimize traffic, and perfecting personalized product recommendations.

DEEP LEARNING

As we increasingly rely on algorithms that can learn on their own, one of the techniques used to improve their performance is deep learning. Deep learning algorithms analyze features of data sets one at a time, developing deeper and deeper layers of analysis, hence the name. This technique can be applied to each of the three learning styles described above.

If I show the picture of a puppy to a deep learning algorithm, it will analyze a feature at a time. It starts with the first layer, perhaps color. Based on the prevalent color, the algorithm determines the probability of it being a puppy. The next layer will perhaps be the presence of a certain shape (i.e., perhaps a shape similar to an eye or a puppy nose) and associate probability with that, the next layer may be texture (i.e., does it look furry?), and so on.

Deep learning is inspired by human neural structures, which are organized in layers. So, many of its applications are called neural networks. If AI imitates the structure of the human brain, you may be tempted to conclude that it is intelligent after all.

Not so fast.

IT'S NOT INTELLIGENT, BUT IT LEARNS

Let's turn back to the case of Google Translate. The system had to learn how to consistently translate among many languages. To accomplish this goal, the system needed to see hundreds of variations of each sentence and hundreds of variations of the correct translation to learn the statistical association between the two. A three-year-old can learn to translate a sentence between French and Chinese after hearing it just a few times, but the algorithm needs to see it many more times to make a reliable connection. The fact that the system needs a statistical model to calculate the probability of a correct sentence translation means, in this respect, the system is not actually intelligent by human standards.

While AI as we know it is not really intelligent, it is a genuine and meaningful example of learning. Learning for lifeforms means a change in behavior following an experience. This is precisely what algorithms do. When they receive more data, their performance becomes more accurate.

THE TURING TEST

Also known as the imitation game, the Turing Test was developed in the 1950s by Alan Turing. The test poses the following question: if you were in a room and communicating simultaneously with two entities in different rooms, such that you could not see them, would you be able to tell, based on their responses, which one of them is a person and which one is actually a machine?

If you are unable to differentiate the level of the responses as human or machine, the machine has passed the Turing Test. How a human answers this question has become standard in determining the effectiveness of artificial intelligence.

BIG DATA

Since the most common Learning Systems can only learn by having a large number of examples, their performance is dependent on the amount of data available. Today, we are collecting more data than ever about people and the world around us. All this data is becoming more accessible due to our increased ability to capture, store, and analyze it in real time, and these Learning Systems need enormous amounts of data in order to be trained to develop an association between an input and an output.

While the term is ubiquitous, the exact meaning of Big Data is not obvious. Of course, 'big' refers to the amount of data we have access to. This amount is actually tiny by comparison with the data we will have access to in only a few years. Besides, there are other features that make Big Data more than just large amounts of data. As Professors Erik Brynjolfsson and Andrew McAfee discuss in their book *The Second Machine Age*, Big Data is defined by four Vs.[3]

VOLUME

An estimated 90 percent of all data stored worldwide has been collected in the last two years. This isn't because we weren't collecting data previously—it's because we now know how to collect more data, faster. In the next couple of years, we will collect more data than we previously have

---

3   Erik Brynjolfsson and Andrew McAfee, *The Second Machine Age: Work, Progress, and Prosperity in a Time of Brilliant Technologies* (New York: W. W. Norton & Company, 2014).

in all of human history. By some estimates, a company like Walmart gathers data equivalent to half a billion filing cabinets worth of text *every hour.*

VELOCITY

Velocity refers to the speed at which data is generated, and, consequently, the speed at which you need to analyze and respond to it. For example, an airplane might have three or four hundred sensors collecting a constant flow of data on its operations during a flight. Even an experienced engineer wouldn't be able to process all that information in a timely manner.

VARIETY

The various data points we collect are different from one another. For example, if someone were to track me exclusively, they would have access to my geolocation information from my GPS, financial data about my spending habits, social data from social media, data on which websites I visit and how often, audio captures, text messages, and closed-circuit surveillance videos. All this information is far too different in format to be analyzed with any one simple technique.

VERACITY

The last V is veracity, or the accuracy of information. Not all data is trustworthy, so it's important to know what data is truthful and reliable. This creates an entirely new level of challenges in the analysis of big data.

The magnitude of this data makes it such that it cannot be processed through the normal means that we're familiar with so that we can extract valuable information from it. As a human, if you read a text or you receive an invoice, your brain would analyze it with certain frameworks or models and then you would make decisions based on those contexts. We cannot do the same with Big Data because of the volume, speed, and variety at which we receive that information make our existing frameworks unfit for such tasks. This is the domain of Learning Systems.

According to the MIT Sloan Management Review,[4] the convergence of machine learning techniques and big data "has emerged as the single most important development that is shaping the future of how firms drive business value from their data and analytics capabilities."

How does data power Learning Systems?

DATA IS THE NEW OIL—AND EVEN MORE

A few years ago, I remember talking with an executive of Zopa, the world's first peer-to-peer lending platform. When I tried to be clever and ask about the strategies of new competitors in the financial industry, he quickly corrected me:

"We are not a financial company. We are a Big Data analytics company, capturing value in the financial sector."

It was a truly eye-opening reply. It taught me that data is not only a bundle of information. It is an input for new

---

4   Randy Bean, "How Big Data is Empowering AI and Machine Learning at Scale," MIT Sloan Management Review, last modified May 8, 2017, https://sloanreview.mit.edu/article/how-big-data-is-empowering-ai-and-machine-learning-at-scale/.

forms of value creation. It is a new type of fuel that powers the 4IR. In other words, data is the new oil.

Data must be extracted, processed, valued, and traded in its own unique way—just like rigs extract oil and pipelines carry it to plants to refine so that consumers can use it for energy. Indeed, there are new businesses models built solely around data collection and exploitation, operated by new "oil companies" of sorts.

Yet, data also differs greatly from oil. For one, it isn't fungible, which means that each data point is unique. A barrel of oil is a barrel of oil is a barrel of oil—but with data, a piece of information about my spending habits last month is not replaceable with a piece of data about someone else's monthly spending habits. In addition, while oil is finite and scarce, the supply of data is limited only by our capacity to capture and store it. If I burn a barrel of oil, no one else can burn that same barrel. The same doesn't apply to data—once it's used, it can be used again. In fact, it can be copied, pasted, and sold to someone else. By combining data with other data, you create additional data that may be even more valuable. The more you use it, the more of it you have, and the more valuable it becomes.

Imagine a barrel of oil that, when you set it aflame, doesn't burn. Instead, new oil gushes out of it. That's data.

In order to take advantage of the data that powers these business models, companies must have a system in place. They have to be aware of the value of data and then implement methodologies to systematically gather it. They then need to have a strategy to transform all of this data into valuable information. Learning Systems have the unique ability to take the information that you *do* have and generate the information you don't. They take the data, analyze it, and then extract meaning from this data that lets you make better decisions than you would have without it.

NETFLIX

Netflix utilizes this to great effect. The company observes the content you have watched and liked, the movies you stopped watching, the moments when you fast-forward or rewind—this is data to them. They gather it, analyze it, and extract information about the content you enjoy. Using that data, they automatically adjust additional information—such as other content that you'd have a high probability of watching. In other words, each user enjoys a uniquely customized Netflix experience.

This customization is based on large amounts of data, because they don't just aggregate information from you as an individual user. They analyze all of the content consumed by all users. They make a prediction so to speak, but they also manage to create information about the probability of what you'd like that would be impossible to accumulate without Learning Systems.

In 2013[5], Netflix stated that "there are thirty-three million different versions of Netflix." At the time, they had thirty-three million subscribers.

---

[5] David Carr, "Giving Viewers What They Want," *The New York Times*, last modified February 24, 2013, https://www.nytimes.com/2013/02/25/business/media/for-house-of-cards-using-big-data-to-guarantee-its-popularity.html.

As Netflix now has 150 million[6] subscribers, one would imagine it offers 150 million different versions. That would overlook the observation that data shows[7] "different viewing behavior depending on the day of the week, the time of the day, the device, and sometimes even the location." Moreover, they constantly test different recommendations to different users, in order to gauge which one works best. This means that Netflix now has *more* versions of itself than it has subscribers.[8]

They also leverage the information to plan and produce new content. The world-famous series "House of Cards" was developed on the basis of viewers' ratings. The theme, the lead actor, and the director had already been validated by millions of users.[9]

How can you leverage Learning Systems to generate business value from data?

---

6   Felix Richter, "International Markets Fuel Netflix Subscriber Growth," Statista, last modified October 17, 2019, https://www.statista.com/chart/10311/netflix-subscriptions-usa-international/.

7   Tom Vanderbilt, "The Science Behind the Netflix Algorithms That Decide What You'll Watch Next," *Wired*, last modified August 7, 2013, https://www.wired.com/2013/08/qq-netflix-algorithm/.

8   Matt Burgess, "This is How Netflix's Secret Recommendation System Works," *Wired*, last modified August 18, 2018, https://www.wired.co.uk/article/netflix-data-personalisation-watching.

9   David Carr, "Giving Viewers What They Want," *The New York Times*, last modified February 24, 2013, https://www.nytimes.com/2013/02/25/business/media/for-house-of-cards-using-big-data-to-guarantee-its-popularity.html.

CLASSIFICATION, PREDICTION, AND GENERATION

In its raw form, data has no value. It's completely dependent on analysis and interpretation to create value. There are three types of tasks that make data meaningful and so, valuable.

For example, when I see my wife, I recognize her in an instant. I cannot tell you how exactly I know she is my wife by seeing her face. I can't tell you about the multiple data points stored in my memory that match what I observe with my eyes, which are my sensors. I have an unaware system to process visual data and classify it as "wife." Various types of Learning Systems can achieve the same result. An example is in anti-spam filters, as mentioned above. When a person sends you an email with certain characteristics, the system classifies it as unwelcomed and sends it to spam. With the same principle, an algorithm can detect anomalies in a product by analyzing its features and classifying it as faulty, which is incredibly useful for manufacturing and quality control.

Another valuable use of data is prediction. For example, I've learnt over time that my wife loves to receive colorful flowers as a surprise gift and red roses on special occasions. So, I can predict her reactions next time I bring her a bouquet. Learning Systems can do the same, in a much more advanced way. This can be used to discover the features of existing customers and predict who are the people most likely to become new customers, using certain patterns of behavior. In addition, by analyzing data sets that have occurred in the past, an algorithm can predict the next data point in a series. This gives us the ability to predict what's coming next. Google does this by auto-completing text that we type into a search box based on keywords we use. Prediction also allows for continuous estimations, such as predicting how heavy traffic on a server will be during a given period. By estimating the amount of energy consumption and heat generated, the algorithm can tell the server how fast the fans need to spin to keep the machine cool.

An extension of this idea comes in the shape of a third task: generation. This is, in many ways, the most interesting, because when this phenomenon occurs, it appears as though the machines have become creative. The trait of creativity is deeply associated with humans and is one of the characteristics associated with intelligence. Because of this, when a machine appears to create independently, people conjure visions of malevolent computers taking over the world.

That said, based on data pulled from past events, an algorithm can create an entirely new data point. These kinds of algorithms are capable of writing articles from scratch based on what they've learned from other, similar articles. They can even compose music, create videos, write speeches, and create missing points in a series, such as in DNA sequencing. If an algorithm is trained with a large number of cat photos, the algorithm can then create a new image that *looks* like a cat but does not come from an actual real cat.[10] It might even be a non-existent species.

---

10 https://thiscatdoesnotexist.com/.

The generative properties of Learning Systems can also benefit optimization processes. Based on certain classifications and predictions, and the number of available inputs, an algorithm will recommend certain behaviors. Take for example the way Uber utilizes Google Maps to tell their drivers where to go. It is based on the starting point combined with real time data about the traffic, road closures, and accidents, along with the final destination. With all of that information, it calculates the most optimal route for the driver to follow. Sometimes it is a route that has never been taken before.

THE END GOAL: NATURAL LANGUAGE PROCESSING

One of the major goals for improving Learning Systems involves a human's ability to communicate with machines in a more fluid manner. Natural Language Processing, or NLP, is a computer's ability to understand the way humans communicate in natural, written, or spoken language, as opposed to computer language, or code.

To perform NLP, a program needs to do three things.

First, it must interpret the meaning of a sentence. It accomplishes this task via a deep learning algorithm that classifies different bits of sound. The program doesn't process the entire sentence, but rather processes sequences of different wavelengths to predict the meaning of a word.

It then decodes the relationship between these pieces and associates it with certain tags that have been identified before in a supervised learning process.

Lastly, it generates a meaningful reply, which is converted into natural sounding speech or actions. Many people are familiar with Siri, Cortana, or Alexa—all systems of AI that already use NLP with good results.

The most promising short-term use of this tech has taken the shape of chatbots. You may encounter a chatbot when interacting with a company's customer service center online. Interestingly enough, you may not know if you are talking to a bot or a human. You may even begin the conversation with a bot and be switched to a human once the conversation becomes more involved. Ideally, the chatbot can understand natural human typing rather than the person needing to type in a way that the bot can understand. This tech is also useful for machine-generated translations and conversational searches, which is what Cortana and Alexa already accomplish.

APPLICATIONS OF LEARNING SYSTEMS

There is an increasing amount of interest and investment in Learning Systems, but most companies don't yet understand how to properly leverage the technology because they don't have a full understanding of how it operates and, perhaps more importantly, its limitations. The functions and applications of Learning Systems are generated from statistical correlations between data points gathered from big data. In other words, these systems don't *understand* anything they do. Instead, they're simply performing applications of statistical methods developed for certain types of data.

As we discussed, this technology is useful for tasks involving classification, prediction, and generation. The first challenge is having the right data and choosing the right algorithm for the task at hand. Therefore, the right data needs to be processed correctly—an often complicated and expensive task. If you give the learning system wrong, incomplete, or biased data, this bias or incompleteness will be replicated forever and reinforced over time, or, as data scientists summarize the concept: "Garbage in, garbage out."

With the right data and algorithms, what can a company do? According to Thomas Davenport of Babson College and Rajeev Ronanki of Deloitte Consulting,[11] there are three broad types of applications.

- *Robotic Process Automation.* The simplest application consists of software imitating repetitive human activities. For example, they can process the incoming orders from clients, sending the corresponding requests to relevant departments, verify that the correct payment has been received, issue an invoice, activate a service, and authorize customer support; they can transfer information from a source (e.g., an email or a form) to a database or across

---

11 Thomas H. Davenport and Rajeev Ronanki, "Artificial Intelligence for the Real World," *Harvard Business Review* (January–February 2018), accessed October 24, 2019, https://hbr.org/2018/01/artificial-intelligence-for-the-real-world.

databases; or they can generate periodic reports based on stored data and highlight areas for intervention or extrapolate trends. Since these are software without any physical component, as discussed above, they are not really "robotic" processes and, since the systems are programmed to repeat a task without any learning, they are barely intelligent. Nonetheless, time-consuming activities can be performed automatically without supervision and with fewer mistakes. Therefore, these systems generate quick returns on investments.

- *Cognitive Insight.* These are Learning Systems that detect consistent patterns in large amounts of data and improve over time, which we discussed above. For example, it can fine-tune the targeting of digital ads or it can predict what a customer will probably like based on the previous purchase behavior of the customer and of other customers who are similar in some relevant characteristics.

- *Cognitive Engagement.* The most advanced, and least common, applications offer complex support to humans, using NLP chatbots. For example, they can respond to customers in their native language, offering technical support, issuing new passwords, or accepting the request to block a credit card and issuing a new one.

Considering the range of capabilities and applications of Learning Systems, it is not surprising that they have been embraced across industries and across corporate functions. In fact, there are now thousands of successful case studies,[12] with stellar outcomes.

A New York dealership of the iconic American motorbike Harley Davidson[13] improved sales by 750 percent in a week and lead generation by almost 3,000 percent in three months. The Spanish energy company Repsol is targeting an increased margin of 30 cents[14] on each barrel of refined oil. Dubai Airport, the world's busiest for international travel, reduced passenger wait time by 30 percent per year[15] since introducing a new real-time data processing system. These are examples of companies whose results have dramatically improved by intelligently deploying Learning Systems.

Others run business models that are not simply improved, but whose value proposition is essentially based on Learning Systems. For example, the Colombian last-mile delivery startup Kiwibot[16] operates a fleet of semi-autonomous food

---

12 www.alelanteri.com

13 Brad Power, "How Harley Davidson Used Artificial Intelligence to Increase New York Sales Leads by 2,930%" *Harvard Business Review*, last modified May 30, 2017, https://hbr.org/2017/05/how-harley-davidson-used-predictive-analytics-to-increase-new-york-sales-leads-by-2930.

14 Anjli Raval, "Google and Repsol Team up to Boost Oil Refinery Efficiency." *Financial Times*, last modified June 3, 2018, https://www.ft.com/content/5711812c-670c-11e8-b6eb-4acfcfb08c11.

15 "New Dubai Airport System to Cut Down Waiting, Travel Time," *Khaleej Times*, last modified July 9, 2019, https://www.khaleejtimes.com/business/aviation/new-dubai-airport-system-to-cut-down-waiting-travel-time.

16 Devin Coldewey, "Kiwi's Food Delivery Bots are Rolling Out to 12 More Colleges," TechCrunch, last modified April 25, 2019,...

delivery vehicles. It is already serving a dozen college campuses in the United States. The Chinese financial services provider and the world's largest fintech company Ant Finance[17] uses Learning Systems "in almost every corner" of its business model. For example, it launched a new screen insurance targeted at young female customers who like to wear tight jeans, after learning that they have their smartphone screens replaced more frequently than other demographics. It developed an automatic insurance claim system based on image recognition that lets clients file a claim by simply uploading a photo taken with their smartphone. It also improved operational efficiency in asset management by 70 percent,[18] while reducing costs by 50 percent, and increasing three-fold the sums invested by returning customers. In fact, rather than a financial company, it is really an AI company creating and capturing value in financial services. As market conditions in China are changing, it is poised to shift to tech services.[19]

What do all these and thousands more similar examples mean for you and your company?

...https://techcrunch.com/2019/04/25/kiwis-food-delivery-bots-are-rolling-out-to-12-new-colleges/.

17 Will Knight, "Meet the Chinese Finance Giant That's Secretly an AI Company," MIT Technology Review, last modified June 16, 2017, https://www.technologyreview.com/s/608103/ant-financial-chinas-giant-of-mobile-payments-is-rethinking-finance-with-ai/.

18 Wang Yanfei, "Ant Financial Opens AI Services to Asset Management Firms," China Daily, last modified June 20, 2018, http://www.chinadaily.com.cn/a/201806/20/WS5b29ee73a3103349141dd4f4.html.

19 "Ant Financial is Shifting its Focus from Finance to Tech Services: Sources," CNBC, last modified June 5, 2018, https://www.cnbc.com/2018/06/05/ant-financial-is-shifting-its-focus-from-finance-to-tech-services-sources.html.

THIS IS THE END OF YOUR INDUSTRY

Think about Uber. What industry does it operate in? Transport or food delivery? Is Tesla a car maker or an energy storage company? Does Airbnb operate in hospitality or experiences? Is LinkedIn a recruitment or a training company? If you answered "both" to these questions, it's clear that these emerging companies no longer define their business model according to their supposed industry.

Did you know that Facebook is now also becoming a payment company?[20] That Amazon earns 10 percent of its revenues from cloud computing[21] solutions? That Google is investing heavily in healthcare?[22] These companies identify new opportunities where their ability to leverage data creates unique value to customers.

The data most companies collect is in excess of their immediate needs. Once such excess data becomes available, however, it can and will be used to create even more value. In doing so, the notion of value creation upstages that of industry.

This is not only the end of your industry. It is the end of the *notion* of an industry.

---

20 Josh Constine, "Facebook Announces Libra Crypocurrency: All You Need to Know," TechCrunch, last modified June 18, 2019, https://techcrunch.com/2019/06/18/facebook-libra/.

21 Jordan Novet, "Amazon Web Services Reports 45 Percent Jump in Revenue in the Fourth Quarter," CNBC, last modified February 1, 2019, https://www.cnbc.com/2019/01/31/aws-earnings-q4-2018.html.

22 Taylor Lorenz, "Google's Investment Arm Spent a Ton of Money on Healthcare This Year," Business Insider, last modified December 16, 2014, https://www.businessinsider.com/google-ventures-invested-over-a-third-of-its-money-in-healthcare-in-2014-2014-12.

Research by McKinsey[23] on the business impact of data analytics reveals that one-third of CEOS worry about cross-sector dynamics. Many are specifically concerned that "companies from other industries have clearer insight into their customers than they do."

As one of the most influential venture capitalists in Silicon Valley, Marc Andreesen, once wrote:[24] "Software is eating the world. In the future every company will be a software company." When he wrote this, in 2011, it was a prediction. In the Fourth Industrial Revolution, it is reality.[25] The examples above show that Netflix is not a media or entertainment company. It is a data analytics company; whose core services are customization and recommendation.[26]

As usual, this is not only a threat, but an opportunity. For example, the law firm Fasken has developed, in house, an AI-powered software to automate legal tasks, such as proofreading legal documents and searching for precedents. The

---

23 Venkat Atluri, Miklós Dietz, and Nicolaus Henke, "Competing in a World of Sectors without Borders," *McKinsey Quarterly* (July 2017), accessed October 21, 2019, https://www.mckinsey.com/business-functions/mckinsey-analytics/our-insights/competing-in-a-world-of-sectors-without-borders.

24 Marc Andreessen, "Why Software Is Eating The World" *The Wall Street Journal*, last modified August 20, 2011, https://www.wsj.com/articles/SB1 0001424053111903480904576512250915629460.

25 Jeetu Patel, "Software Is Still Eating the World," TechCrunch, last modified June 7, 2016, https://techcrunch.com/2016/06/07/software-is-eating-the-world-5-years-later/.

26 Mario Gavira, "How Netflix Uses AI and Data to Conquer the World," LinkedIn, last modified July 2, 2018, https://www.linkedin.com/pulse/how-netflix-uses-ai-data-conquer-world-mario-gavira/.

software works so well that Fasken recently launched a spinoff to sell it to other law firms.[27] Companies in other industries are now doing the same.

So, if you woke up today thinking that you work in finance, retail, or manufacturing, I recommend you go to sleep tonight thinking that you work in a software company, operating in the broad field of transforming data into value. To do so successfully, you must embrace Learning Systems.

Ultimately, Learning Systems are a general-purpose technology,[28] or a new method to produce and innovate that creates a paradigm shift across industries. Other examples of similar technologies are steam power, electricity, and the computer—which prompted the previous industrial revolutions. They have different uses, can be applied to many different fields, and trigger many spillover effects. In the next chapter, we will discuss some of these emerging and fast expanding technologies.

QUESTIONS

1. What are some areas where your company could benefit from rapidly classifying new data into relevant categories?

27 Angus Loten, "Our it Is So Good, Lets Sell It, Firms Say," *The Wall Street Journal*, last modified July 9, 2019, https://www.wsj.com/articles/our-it-is-so-good-lets-sell-it-firms-say-11562664603.

28 Boyan Jovanovic and Peter L. Rosseau, "Chapter 18 - General Purpose Technologies," *Handbook of Economic Growth*, Volume 1, Part B (2005): 1181-1224, accessed October 21, 2019, http://www.nyu.edu/econ/user/jovanovi/JovRousseauGPT.pdf.

2. What are some tasks where being able to make more accurate, faster predictions would give you an edge?

3. Do you have enough high-quality, accurate data to train an algorithm so that the classification and prediction tasks it performs are sufficiently accurate?

4. How could you increase the amount of real-time, reliable data you collect and use?

5. Are you worried that one of your competitors might develop a solution based on a Learning System? What solution?

6. Are you worried that a company from a different industry might develop such a solution?

CHAPTER FOUR

EXPONENTIAL TECHNOLOGIES

O ne of the world's most valuable brands until the 1990s, and with a strong grasp on the photography market worldwide, Kodak filed for bankruptcy in 2012.[1] While the company survived, they now operate at a significantly reduced capacity compared to their heyday.

What happened?

---

1   "The Last Kodak Moment?" *The Economist* (January 14, 2012), accessed October 21, 2019, https://www.economist.com/business/2012/01/14/the-last-kodak-moment.

Kodak was driven out of business by the rise of digital photography. The ironic part of this story is that most of the patents and technology required for digital photography were filed, and are still owned, by the company. In short, Kodak invented digital photography, only to be driven out of business by its own invention.[2]

Is this even possible?

In the 1970s, Steven Sasson, an engineer at Kodak, and his team invented the first digital camera. The machine was the size of a microwave and took twenty-three seconds to take a single black and white photo. Its resolution was a mere 0.01 megapixels, which was really poor. The photos were stored on cassette, as they were the standard technology for recording digital data. This meant you had to put it in a cassette recorder, connect that recorder to a $5,000 computer, and then connect to a television screen, all to view a 0.01-megapixel black and white photo. Obviously, this technology was not appealing to consumers.

After years of working on improving the digital technology, the team had increased the resolution several times, and the improvement was substantial. Even then, the starting point of the technology was so low that the level of improvement was practically undetectable. If you have a 0.01-megapixel resolution and you double it, it only becomes 0.02—doubling it twice more only takes you to 0.08. Each doubling took years of research and investment.

2   Jordan Crook, "What Happened To Kodak's Moment?" TechCrunch, last modified January 21, 2012, https://techcrunch.com/2012/01/21/what-happened-to-kodaks-moment/.

So, it appeared as though the technology was not going to make strides for several decades.

Knowing what we do today, we can say that this was a massive mistake—so much so that "the Kodak moment" is now short for any cautionary tale of sudden disruption.

How could Kodak have missed what was coming?

Until the late 1990s, Kodak held a very pessimistic outlook on demand for digital cameras.[3] It also did not want to take away any market share from analogic photography. So, with other traditional photography products selling so well, Kodak decided this technology was not worth pursuing further.

THE IMPACT OF TECHNOLOGICAL IMPROVEMENT

My parents are both physicians. In the 1990s, they used to spend a significant amount of time volunteering in Africa, raising funds to support hospitals and donating medicines. During their time working there, they also traveled the continent. They returned from one such trip extremely excited because they had taken photos of a unique event—it was raining in the Namib, a desert where it only rained every thirty years or so—and they had captured it on film. They took the film to be developed—and the place that processed the film accidentally destroyed it, losing the pictures forever. What a disappointment! Even when films were not ruined, in the 1990s getting photos developed cost time and

3   Dave Lehmkuhl, Jeff Liebl, Larry Lien, and Sherleen Ong, "Kodak: The Challenge of Consumer Digital Camera," accessed October 21, 2019, http://www-personal.umich.edu/~afuah/cases/case9.html.

money. Once the photos were developed, they could only be shown in person to the people nearby. If my parents wanted anyone else to see their photos, they would have had to obtain further copies and mail them to friends.

The whole process has changed, and it's not just about the technology itself. Now, if my parents were in the desert while it was raining, they could take multiple photos, apply a variety of different filters to make the pictures look perfect. They could identify the photo as being taken by them, in a certain location on a certain day and time, and share it with anyone on the planet. They could also make sure that people only see it once and then destroy it if they so desired.

All of this now is possible in seconds, and for free.

The *change* and the *speed* at which these things change now is such that it defies imagination. The way it occurred in the digital photography realm is an excellent example of what we now call Exponential Technologies. Simply put, Exponential Technologies are those that are improving not at a constant, but at an accelerating speed.

EXPONENTIAL GROWTH

The phenomenon of exponential growth was initially described by Gordon Moore,[4] one of the founders of Intel. Moore noticed that in the early 1960s, computer processors doubled their computing power while becoming half as big

---

4   "Moore's Law," Oxford Reference, accessed October 21, 2019, https://www.oxfordreference.com/view/10.1093/oi/authority.20110803100208256.

and half as expensive every eighteen to twenty-four months. He pointed out this phenomenon in what is now called Moore's Law, a concept we mentioned earlier in the book. At the time, Moore believed this would only continue for a few more years. Instead, it has been happening for decades now. Technology has continued roughly doubling in performance and halving in size and cost.[5]

Ray Kurzweil, the director of engineering at Google and a co-founder of the think tank Singularity University, recognized that Moore's law applies not only to processors but to all digital technologies. He thus extended it and called the new law The Law of Accelerating Returns.[6] In short, Kurzweil says that the performance and capacity of any information-enabled technology progresses at a predictable, exponential rate, across the three dimensions of performance, size, and cost.

Figure 3 compares the linear pattern of an analogic technology—think fuel efficiency as mentioned in the introduction—to the exponential trajectory of digital technologies.

This speed of growth is hard for the human brain to truly comprehend, and therefore it's difficult to account for when making strategic decisions. Kurzweil broke it down, however, by examining what Exponential Technologies have in common. They all go through six stages of development:

5   Béla Nagy, J. Doyne Farmer, Quan M. Bui, and Jessika E. Trancik, "Statistical Basis for Predicting Technological Progress," *PLoS ONE* 8, no. 2 (February 28, 2013), accessed October 9, 2019, https://journals.plos.org/plosone/article?id=10.1371/journal.pone.0052669.

6   Ray Kurzweil (2001). The Law of Accelerating Returns. Kurzweil AI. https://www.kurzweilai.net/the-law-of-accelerating-returns

digitization, deceptive growth, disruptive growth, dematerialization, demonetization, and democratization. Recognizing these stages can help you identify technologies that
are at the tipping point for exponential growth and use that
knowledge to build your business strategy.

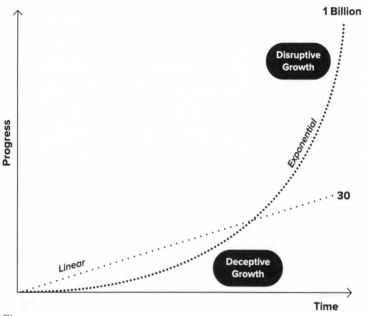

Figure 3.

DIGITIZATION

The first stage is digitization. Digitization happens when a
physical product or process is transformed into software
or code. When a new technology becomes information-enabled, it goes into a trajectory of exponential growth. When
Sasson created the digital camera, as clunky as it was, he set
this process in motion.

DECEPTIVE GROWTH

Once Kodak began the process of digitization, digital photography began improving in every dimension. Initially, the digital camera weighed three kilograms, was very slow, and had a poor resolution. Soon it became faster, cheaper, and the resolution improved. However, because their starting point was so poor, the exponential rate did not appear remarkable enough to warrant investments. Kodak could not see the emerging exponential pattern. This stage of growth is "deceptive."

DISRUPTIVE GROWTH

Disruptive growth comes seemingly out of nowhere. For years, Kodak concentrated on traditional cameras, which were steadily growing and improving over time. The demand for digital cameras was small at first, because the technology was simply not on par with what traditional cameras could do, and Kodak predicted it would remain a niche for many years.

As a result, the company was blindsided when the demand for digital cameras suddenly exploded. Digital technology had been slowly improving until it reached the tipping point where the technology was good enough to justify the cost. For digital cameras, this happened in the mid-1990s when the quality finally approached one megapixel. Suddenly, it created competition with the established analogic technology.

There is a critical point between deceptive and disruptive growth. When the digital technology becomes good enough to be comparable to the analogic one, the analog technology is doomed, because at that point, the difference in speed of improvements accelerates. Traditional technologies keep growing, but at a linear rate. Indeed, traditional photography kept getting better, but there was a point when the exponential growth of digital equaled it in performance and, shortly after, vastly improved and outcompeted it.

Analog technologies survive as niche products for amateurs. People still listen to vinyl records and take photos with film cameras, but neither are the technical standard any longer.

DEMATERIALIZATION

After this happened, the whole system of technology changed. Not only did the higher resolution photos get cheaper, but the size of the technology continued to decrease. The physics of the value creation changed because the core of the value creation moved to a piece of software with almost no physical component. This is the stage of dematerialization.

Because software has no material component, value creation is increasingly disconnected from physical manifestation. The smartphone in your pocket now holds a telephone, a flashlight, a radio, a calculator, a few high-resolution cameras, a music player, and a GPS. All of this technology occupied a whole room in 1980—and some of it was simply unavailable to consumers. Think about the GPS. In 1980 it was a tall antenna to be found only in a military compound—it was a military-grade technology then. Now, once again, it's so tiny you can't see it and it's so cheap *it comes with* the smartphone.

DEMONETIZATION

Indeed, with software being replicated so cheaply and limitlessly, the price of technology drops to almost zero.

Making additional copies of a physical item is expensive. If manufacturing a smartphone costs $100, manufacturing two costs $200, and so on. With large numbers of smartphones, there will be some savings thanks to economies of scale. However, the cost can never approach zero, because physical production requires facilities, labor, utilities, raw materials, logistics...and these are not free. On the other hand, every additional identical copy of a software is created instantaneously—and free.

The average smartphone nowadays packs technology so advanced that, in the 1980s, the same technology would have cost $1 million![7] Most of us barely notice, because it's now so cheap. Digital cameras, the technology that brought Kodak to its knees, don't even truly exist as standalone objects anymore. They are still available for sale but are increasingly reserved for niche users. Why buy a separate camera when several of increasingly high quality now *come with* your smartphone?

DEMOCRATIZATION

Democratization is the last stage, where almost everyone in society has access to the technology due to the demonetization and affordability of the product. Digital cameras are not luxury items anymore. Thanks to the democratization of the technology, it's almost standard and broadly possessed.

---

7   Peter H. Diamandis and Steven Kotler, *Abundance: The Future is Better Than You Think* (New York: Free Press, 2012).

There are currently almost eight billion[8] mobile phone subscriptions worldwide, more than one per person on the planet! The figure should not suggest that everybody has a mobile phone. Unfortunately, there is still a large gap between rich and progressive countries like the UAE, where residents own on average more than two mobile phones each, and less advanced ones, like Congo DRC,[9] where there is only one mobile phone per four residents. These are not all smartphones. Yet, soon 40 percent[10] of the world population will have a smartphone, albeit with the same gap between countries.

What does this mean for your business?

BELLWETHERS

You have no option but to stay ahead of the curve on Exponential Technologies.

Digital technologies improve and expand at an accelerating pace, such that the companies that depend on old technologies go out of business very quickly—too quickly for laggards to catch up. We've seen this pattern happen time and time again in the music, video, and telephone industries, among others.

8 "Mobile Subscriptions Q1 2019," Ericsson, accessed October 21, 2019, https://www.ericsson.com/en/mobility-report/reports/june-2019/mobile-subscriptions-q1-2019.

9 "The Mobile Economy: Sub-Saharan Africa 2017," GSM Association (2017), accessed October 21, 2019, https://www.gsmaintelligence.com/research/?file=7bf3592e6d750144e58d9dcfac6adfab&download.

10 Arne Holst, "Smartphone User Penetration as Percentage of Total Global Population from 2014 to 2021," Statista, last modified May 31, 2019, https://www.statista.com/statistics/203734/global-smartphone-penetration-per-capita-since-2005/.

So, be on the lookout for the tipping point when technology reaches the critical state where it's good enough to replace the pre-existing analogic technology. This is a slow and subtle process, so most people don't see it coming and fail to prepare. They have already been desensitized over the long years of hype and unfulfilled promises.

Part of locating and recognizing deceptive growth comes from looking at which goods and services are in the process of being digitized—or, even better, what has not yet been digitized and could be. Recognizing it early on allows companies the chance to not just project but to own the change. Kodak nearly accomplished this, but mistakenly believed that technology improvement and adoption rate would keep at the ongoing deceptive growth pace.

This was not only Kodak's mistake. One of the world's most reputable consulting companies, McKinsey had reportedly[11] made a similar mistake in 1980. When the phone company AT&T asked McKinsey to forecast the number of cellphone users by the year 2000, the answer was: nine hundred thousand. So, AT&T decided against costly investments in the new technology—which, incidentally, it had invented.

By the year 2000, the actual number of cellphone users was 109 million. As seen, the figure is now higher than the world population.

---

11 Àngel Lozano, "1) Cellular Telephony: Just a Niche Market," Universitat Pumpeu Febra, last modified March 25, 2019, https://www.upf.edu/web/angel-lozano/innovation/-/asset_publisher/AZaAOTtL3c4Z/content/id/223464268/maximized.

AT&T and Kodak serve as cautionary tales for failing to understand Exponential Technologies. As discussed before, however, improved technology is only the first step. When many people carry such advanced technology in their back pockets, new business models become possible. Then entire industries are redesigned. Then the whole world changes.

It took less than forty years to put $1 million worth of 1980 technology in most people's pockets. Yet, thanks to exponential improvements, putting the equivalent amount of today's technology in most people's pockets will take much less—less than fifteen years.

Just imagine what becomes possible then.

It is this speed of change that businesses need to be aware of in order to capitalize on opportunities. If most people have this technology at their fingertips in fifteen years and your company isn't prepared for it, you will be, for all intents and purposes, an old company—outdated because you didn't keep up with the technology.

Yet, the excitement for a new technology may not be a good enough reason for you to jump on the bandwagon. Investments in early technologies are expensive and often fail.

How can you time your entry smartly?

INDICATORS OF DISRUPTION

Gideon Gartner, the founder of the IT advisory firm Gartner Group, conceptualized a cycle the describes the lifecycle of hype around new technology.

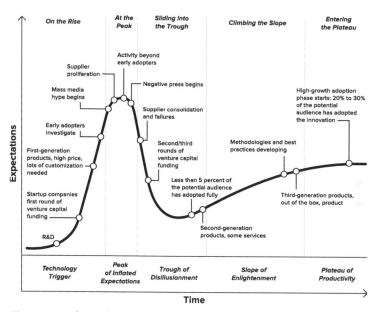

Figure 4. cc Olga Tarkovskiy (2013)

Figure 4 shows the hype cycle.[12] According to Gartner, at the beginning, a new technology's quality and visibility are low. Only researchers and technology fanatics are aware of it during the *Technology Trigger* stage. As early proof-of-concept demonstrations receive attention and early investments start to flow in, there is a rapid growth in visibility—too rapid, relative to the advancement of the technology. This is the stage Gartner calls *Inflated Expectations*. For example, for years, the media has been hyping the 3-D printer as an advancement in manufacturing technology that will change the landscape of the industry. Many people

---

12 "Gartner Hype Cycle," Gartner, accessed October 24, 2019, https://www.gartner.com/en/research/methodologies/gartner-hype-cycle.

have heard about this technology, and their expectations have been inflated far beyond—at least at the time of writing this book—what the technology is in fact capable of.

As experiments in the new technology keep failing and implementation lags, interest quickly wanes. To be sure, the technology keeps improving at a deceptively exponential rate. Yet, the public becomes disillusioned, disbelieving the tech will ever benefit them. As a result, visibility decreases quickly as people move on to the next shiny thing. For example, between 2013 and 2014, when Google launched the first set of smart glasses with augmented reality (AR) features, it was all the rage[13] among the technology gurus and influencers of Silicon Valley. Yet, the glasses still had a buggy performance[14] and raised severe privacy[15] concerns. Soon they were proclaimed dead. Less than a year after launch, Google stopped selling them.

Or did it?

After a hiatus, Google pivoted the glasses to industrial applications. Most people have not heard about this. They still think that Google Glass folded. This is the stage Gartner calls the *Trough of Disillusionment*, when the technology

---

13 Henry Blodget, "Silicon Valley Tech Gods Are So Excited About Their Google Glasses They Can't Stop Talking About Them," *Business Insider*, last modified April 30, 2013, http://www.businessinsider.com/loic-lemeur-google-glass-2013-4.

14 Jay Yarow, "The Verdict Is In: Nobody Likes Google Glass," *Business Insider*, last modified May 3, 2013, http://www.businessinsider.com/nobody-really-likes-google-glass-2013-5.

15 Daniel Thomas, "UK Watchdog Raises Privacy Concerns over Google Glass," *Financial Times*, last modified June 26, 2014, http://www.ft.com/content/3488b1d2-fd59-11e3-96a9-00144feab7de.

keeps progressing, but receives very little attention—after failing to deliver against unrealistic, *Inflated Expectations*.

Yet, as the technology becomes better understood, second and third generation improvements are released. Applications become viable and they are rolled out to productive use. This is where Google Glasses presently are. They have dozens of applications across the value chain, from product development to after-sale services, and across industries, from healthcare to manufacturing. Companies such as Boeing, DHL, and General Electric are using them. This stage is called *Slope of Enlightenment*. For digital technologies, this stage tends to overlap with the beginning of *Disruptive Growth*.

Finally, the technology becomes reliable. Multiple providers release differentiated offerings, mainstream adoption starts, and the market continues to grow. The technology reaches a *Plateau of Productivity*. Yet, by now it no longer attracts much attention, as it's been around long enough to have exhausted its novelty.

Eventually, the technology begins to mature to the tipping point between deceptive and disruptive growth. This is when visibility increases again, with all the same inflated claims.

So, when should you enter the game?

According to the chairman of X-Prize Foundation and co-founder of Singularity University, Peter Diamandis, and the author Steven Kotler, there is a simple and elegant way to identify this key moment of transition between deceptive and disruptive growth. In their book *Bold*, they suggest it's when the technology is no longer exclusive to geeks but available to entrepreneurs and the public. Three-dimensional printing, AI, and cybersecurity are already in this disruptive growth stage and are already successfully reimagining entire industries.

NEW TECHS ON THE BLOCK

Considering how fast digital technologies emerge and evolve, I was very lucky to be introduced to them at what at the time was considered a very young age. My father has always been a proponent of investing in new technologies and knowledge. So, he bought me my first personal computer when I was five years old. The screen had only two colors—light green and dark green, and it was, quite frankly, awful. Any time I wanted to do anything with it, I had to type in a number of odd lines to give the computer a command. In order to give this command, however, I first had to navigate the directory of where different software and content were organized within the computer so that I could give a certain set of orders to get the computer to perform. As user-unfriendly as that was, it was even less convenient for people to interact with computers in the time prior to the early home machines. Users then were required to use punch cards to interface with the digital world.

Of course, this would improve. In the 1980s, Apple developed an operating system with a graphical interface and the mouse. Suddenly, instead of typing long lines of code, you could grab a piece of plastic with your hand, drag it around your desk, and control the arrow moving around on your screen.

Most of you would consider this absolutely normal now—second nature and intuitive. It feels natural to you because you have already done it for an extended period of time. For some of you, it's the only way you've ever known how to interact with a computer. The truth is that it is *not* intuitive. When my mother tried to learn how to use a computer, it took her a few classes to use a mouse. In order to do so, she held the mouse with her right hand, then held on to her right wrist with her left hand and moved her left arm to get the right arm to move the mouse. When the arrow on the screen reached the right spot, she lifted both hands and carefully clicked on the mouse button with her right index finger. Unfortunately, this often resulted in the mouse moving, and the arrow opening the wrong file. All this is not to ridicule my mother's efforts. She's a highly trained and successful (now retired) medical doctor. It's to show how unintuitive and unfriendly this technology could be. Indeed, already this method of interaction is almost obsolete. Most of us use laptops with more intuitive trackpads, and even those are on their way out.

Luckily for her, my mother leapfrogged the mouse and the trackpad, and jumped straight into the new generation. Most of us now are familiar with the idea of a multi-touch-screen, on a mobile phone or tablet, to interact with technology. You'd be surprised at how quickly she can now bring order to our family chat on WhatsApp.

All of these interfaces have one thing in common—they are two-dimensional (2D). Increasingly, that method of interaction is disappearing and a new one is emerging that is more immersive and conversational.

AUGMENTED, VIRTUAL, AND MIXED REALITY

Augmented reality (AR), virtual reality (VR), and mixed reality (MR) transform the 2-D interface into a three-dimensional (3-D) one where you are fully immersed in digital data, to allow you to interact with it in a more intuitive and natural way.[16]

As a result, your cognitive load is reduced. For example, if you're consulting information on a map or the 2-D screen of a GPS, your brain has to make an effort to translate that information into something that happens in the 3-D world. It requires some skill and effort, and we still make mistakes, as you know well if you've ever made a wrong turn while trying to decipher Google Maps. With a 3-D interface, we will soon have an AR windshield where the glass itself would have an arrow saying, "Turn here." This would significantly reduce the effort necessary to interact with the digital world and translate its information into better decisions in the real world.

Google Glass is an example of AR. AR is an interface where you perceive the physical reality of your location at that point in time, with some digital data overlaid on this reality. The digital data is present, but it does not interfere with your perception of the environment.

---

16 "What Comes After Smartphones? The Next Mobile Computing Platform Is Already Emerging," CBInsights, last modified August 21, 2018, https://www.cbinsights.com/research/mobile-computing-platform-future/.

In MR, the data are responsive to the environment. For example, you could have a digital animal that hides behind a real-world tree—think Pokémon Go. Your interface would recognize the tree and be able to place the creature behind it to create a surprise or something that needs to be found. This creates a system where you still experience your physical reality at your location and in your time, but the digital data interacts with it.

Naturally then, VR is such that you no longer perceive your reality—the physical reality of where you are at that time of day. You are completely surrounded by a virtual experience.

These technologies hold an important strategic value[17] for companies. Because they reduce the cognitive load, they allow humans to do more, and faster—to use data in real time. Imagine working as a chef and being able to have your glasses tell you that the oven has reached a certain temperature and that the chicken inside it is cooked—and then being able to look at that oven and telling it through the glasses to switch off. How much more efficient of a chef could you be with those capabilities?

A related technology, accelerating the progress of immersive computing are voice-controlled assistants, such as Siri and Alexa. The visual portion is fast approaching. On its heels will be improved sound experiences that will further

---

17 Michael E. Porter and James E. Heppelmann, "A Manager's Guide to Augmented Reality." *Harvard Business Review* (November-December 2017), accessed October 21, 2019, https://hbr.org/2017/11/a-managers-guide-to-augmented-reality#the-battle-of-the-smart-glasses.

transform the relationship between the physical and the digital world, and our place in it. If these technologies continue to grow at this speed, they will rapidly become the next mainstream computing platform.

PERVASIVE COMPUTING

Unlike my old PC, which operated in isolation, we now have an expansive network of smart connected devices. According to the late Mark Weiser, who first coined the term, ubiquitous, or pervasive computing captures a generation shift in computing. First there were large mainframes, each shared by many users. The current generation are personal computers and devices, each accessed by an individual user. The third generation are computers that fade into the background of our lives. "The most profound technologies are those that disappear,"[18] wrote Weiser.

Pervasive computers take on a further meaning because they are not only hidden. They are also connected, forming what we call the Internet of Things (IoT)[19] or, more ambitiously and perhaps more fittingly, the Internet of Everything.

As for other Exponential Technologies, processors, sensors, and connectivity are becoming better and cheaper at an accelerating pace. We've already mentioned the rapid drop

---

18 Mark Weiser, "The Computer for the 21st Century," last modified June 22, 2018, https://web.archive.org/web/20180622160538/http://www.ubiq. com/hypertext/weiser/SciAmDraft3.html.

19 Peter H. Diamandis, "When the World Is Wired: The Magic of the Internet of Everything," Singularity Hub, last modified January 4, 2018, https://singularityhub.com/2016/02/09/when-the-world-is-wired-the-magic-of-the-internet-of-everything/.

in cost of computational power. Sensor prices have dropped by over 50 percent[20] in ten years and we expect one trillion[21] to be connected by 2020. With 5G, the new generation mobile connectivity standard, the speed of connection is expected to improve one hundred times[22] relative to 4G and its cost will become "essentially free"[23] in the near future.

A noticeable trend in this area has been the expansion of cloud computing. This amounts to an inexpensive service of centralized processors and storage, accessed remotely. For example, when you give a command to Siri or Cortana, your voice is processed by a computer hosted very far away. No matter how fast the computer, the increasing amount of data and the distance it needs to travel causes some delay, or latency. Despite the increasing performance of 5G,[24] the next trend is towards edge computing,[25] or computing done

20 "The Internet of Things: Making Sense of the Next Mega-Trend," The Goldman Sachs Group, Inc., last modified September 3, 2014, https://www.goldmansachs.com/insights/pages/internet-of-things/iot-report.pdf.

21 Vanessa Bates Ramirez, "These Are the Meta-Trends Shaping the Future (at Breakneck Speed)," Singularity Hub, last modified August 20, 2019, https://singularityhub.com/2019/08/20/these-are-the-meta-trends-shaping-the-future-at-breakneck-speed/.

22 Peter H. Diamandis, "4 Billion New Minds Online: The Coming Era of Connectivity," Singularity Hub, last modified July 27, 2018, https://singularityhub.com/2018/07/27/4-billion-new-minds-online-the-coming-era-of-connectivity/.

23 Peter H. Diamandis, "When the World Is Wired: The Magic of the Internet of Everything," Singularity Hub, last modified January 4, 2018, https://singularityhub.com/2016/02/09/when-the-world-is-wired-the-magic-of-the-internet-of-everything/.

24 "What Is 5G? Understanding The Next-Gen Wireless System Set To Enable Our Connected Future." CBInsights, last modified January 23, 2019, https://www.cbinsights.com/research/5g-next-gen-wireless-system/.

25 Paul Miller, "What Is Edge Computing?" The Verge, accessed...

at the source of the data. In other words, the cloud is no longer remote, but distributed.

Billions of wearable and portable devices, vehicles, home appliances, city infrastructures, and industrial machinery are already connected. This ever-expanding network of smart connected devices makes information available anywhere. A critical novelty is that information is no longer stored in private databases, but it is increasingly shared in public networks. A prominent example is the blockchain,[26] which is a decentralized database, shared across a network of computers, where stored information is continuously verified and reconciled, making it very hard to modify without authorization. In this way, digital assets can be transferred without the need for a trusted third party. Entire value chains and business models across dozens of industries are being redesigned.[27]

These smart connected devices are deeply transforming business models[28] and competition,[29] making it possible

---

...October 21, 2019, https://www.theverge.com/circuitbreaker/
2018/5/7/17327584/edge-computing-cloud-google-microsoft-apple-amazon.

26 Don Tapscott and Alex Tapscott, *Blockchain Revolution: How the Technology Behind Bitcoin and Other Cryptocurrencies is Changing the World* (New York: Portfolio, 2018).

27 Paul Miller, "What Is Edge Computing?" The Verge, accessed October 21, 2019, https://www.theverge.com/circuitbreaker/2018/5/7/17327584/edge-computing-cloud-google-microsoft-apple-amazon.

28 Marco Iansiti and Karim R. Lakhani, "Digital Ubiquity: How Connections, Sensors, and Data Are Revolutionizing Business," *Harvard Business Review* (November 2014), accessed October 21, 2019, https://hbr.org/2014/11/digital-ubiquity-how-connections-sensors-and-data-are-revolutionizing-business.

29 Michael E. Porter and James E. Heppelmann, "How Smart, Connected Products Are Transforming Competition," *Harvard*...

to create, deliver, and capture value. Pervasive computing is empowering new ways to generate revenues through products and services that incorporate accurate, real-time information. It also allows substantial efficiencies and cost savings.[30]

3-D PRINTING

It used to be that to create a physical product, you would take a piece of a material and remove parts from it—you take a piece of wood and carve it and shape it into the tool you so desired. In manufacturing, a big technological shift was industrial stamping. You first created a sheet metal and then pressed or cut it into the desired shape. Another advance was injection molding. Here you created a mold, poured a liquid into it, solidified it, and removed it. With both techniques, you would then polish and take any excess material away.

Thanks to advances in chemistry and digital technologies, we can perform additive manufacturing or 3-D printing.[31] Instead of removing material, we add. We start with a

...*Business Review* (November 2014), accessed October 21, 2019, https://hbr.org/2014/11/how-smart-connected-products-are-transforming-competition.

30   "The Internet of Things: Making Sense of the Next Mega-Trend," The Goldman Sachs Group, Inc., last modified September 3, 2014, https://www.goldmansachs.com/insights/pages/internet-of-things/iot-report.pdf.

31   Peter H. Diamandis, "How 3D Printing Is Transforming the Way We Make Things," Singularity Hub, last modified March 7, 2016, https://singularityhub.com/2016/03/07/how-3d-printing-is-transforming-the-way-we-make-things/.

blank slate and slowly accumulate what is needed to build the item or tool. This is done by melting the material, printing the object, and allowing it to solidify. The technology is advancing rapidly, already being able to use materials other than plastic to print, including metals, and even organic tissue. It is possible to print bone and skin for reconstruction. Organ printing is not far from the realm of possibility.

Three-dimensional printing is transforming manufacturing. The potential of this technology is immense. Three-dimensional printers can create extremely complex structures of mixed materials and they allow customization and on-demand production fast and at scale, substantially reducing the need for inventory. Moreover, for some applications, it only employs 10 percent[32] of the raw materials necessary for traditional processes.

From a business perspective, again you must consider what will happen when this technology is available to a large segment of the population at a reasonable price. It means that the value will no longer sit with the physical component of a good—that it will increasingly sit with the digital portion of it. If a customer wants a new mug, instead of going to the store to buy one, she will download the design of a mug she likes and print it in the living room. When that becomes mainstream, every industry that is involved in physical goods will be radically transformed.

---

32 Peter H. Diamandis, "5 Big Breakthroughs to Anticipate in 3D Printing," Singularity Hub, last modified April 8, 2019, https://singularityhub. com/2019/04/08/5-big-breakthroughs-to-anticipate-in-3d-printing/.

BIOTECHNOLOGY

Another technology impacting the physical world affects organic matter itself. Biotechnology refers to the concept of using organisms or some other sort of living system to create new products. For example, certain algae and fungi have been developed to transform waste into fuel.[33] It is also quite common to use biometric information instead of passwords. Yet more interesting, however, is that we are increasingly transferring physical, biological data into digital data, which sends it into exponential growth.

For example, the sequencing of the human genome (DNA),[34] completed in 2003, marked a milestone in healthcare. It proved a formidable challenge, that took thirteen years and cost $2.7 billion. Yet, a mere fifteen years later, sequencing an individual's DNA takes only a few hours and costs about $1,000.[35] At this point, having been familiarized with several Exponential Technologies, this should not come as a surprise. This level of understanding of our DNA is rapidly making possible precision medicine, or an approach to treating disease that is sensitive to each individual genetic

33 Exxon Mobile, "The Future of Energy? It May Come From Where You Least Expect," *The New York Times*, accessed October 21, 2019, https://www.nytimes.com/paidpost/exxonmobil/the-future-of-energy-it-may-come-from-where-you-least-expect.html.

34 "The Human Genome Project," National Human Genome Research Institute, accessed October 21, 2019, https://www.genome.gov/human-genome-project.

35 "Sumit Jamuar: Indians Are 20% of the World's Population, but Represent Only 1% of Existing Genetic Data," LSE Business... ...Review, last modified January 10, 2018, https://blogs.lse.ac.uk/businessreview/2018/01/10/sumit-jamuar-indians-are-20-of-the-worlds-population-but-represent-only-1-of-existing-genetic-data.

profile. Another application of this new knowledge is intervening on DNA itself to modify it. This is possible through a gene-editing technique based on a type of DNA sequence called CRISPR (or Clustered Regularly Interspaced Shorty Palindromic repeats).

One novel phenomenon is insertables.[36] Similar to a microchip for your pets, insertables are implants the size of a grain of rice that are placed in the body. They allow you to use near-field communications—or NCF, which is what we use for contactless payments—to do such things as unlocking your door or paying for something simply by scanning your hand near a sensor. There are implants that allow humans to know their directional orientation—north, south, east, or west, at all times. There are insertables that are small magnets designed to go under our fingertips that let us perceive magnetic fields. There are antennae that can be implanted directly into the skull to allow colorblind people to perceive color correctly, and even detect infrared. There is a liquid that can be injected into your eyes to allow you to see in the dark.

These biological technologies are not without some strong ethical resistances, which might slow down their progress. However, as a business leader, you need to be aware of their exponential growth and trajectory.

---

36 Calla Wahlquist, "Under the Skin: How Insertable Microchips Could Unlock the Future," *The Guardian*, last modified October 31, 2017, https://www.theguardian.com/technology/2017/nov/01/under-the-skin-how-insertable-microchips-could-unlock-the-future.

ALL TOGETHER NOW

When these Exponential Technologies break into the mainstream, they will change the world. Professor Albert Segars[37] predicts that each of these technologies individually will "fundamentally [change] the way we work and consume (commerce), our well-being (health), our intellectual evolution (learning), and the natural world around us (environment)." He also observes that, while it may still be possible to analyze them as separate technologies, they are rapidly converging. What does it mean?

Let's consider healthcare.

Sensors might collect a continuous flow of data from everyone. This data could be stored in a blockchain, to be always truthful and accessible on-demand. It could be also anonymously analyzed, through Learning Systems, to uncover subtle patterns. These patterns could recommend therapeutic interventions, customized for each individual patient's genetic profile. Custom-designed drugs could then be 3-D printed at the patient's house. This series of technological improvements will transform the industry and its business models. Yet more, it will redefine our human experience, for example, of what it means to be ill. In fact, with sufficient data and predictive accuracy, we may not even fall ill ever again. The cycle would then continue. Sensors would share information on how patients respond to treatments.

---

37 Albert H. Segars, "Seven Technologies Remaking the World," MIT Sloan Management Review, last modified March 9, 2018, https://sloanreview. mit.edu/projects/seven-technologies-remaking-the-world/.

Algorithms might design new molecules and drugs at a fraction of the cost of current medical research. This way, patients will lead healthier and longer lives. This will arguably be possible at a negligible cost and so become available to everyone.

It is hard to imagine how the world will look like when most of humanity is healthy. Even if we could imagine it, such a scenario would be very limited. Similar processes will ensure equivalent outcomes in other domains. What will the world look like when everyone is not only healthy, but also has excellent education, free transportation, access to food and water, and unlimited energy? It will be an age of almost utopian abundance[38] and prosperity.

If you miss out on one of these technological advances, it will be quite difficult to catch up, as the speed at which they change is so rapid. The convergence of better data, better algorithms, better computation power, better storage, and better interfaces will drive forward the next waves of technological development. This, in turn, will unleash a new wave of innovations,[39] new business models, and new lifestyles. Therefore, it's so important to stay at the forefront of these emerging technologies.

In the next chapter, we will discuss an old business model, which has been completely revamped thanks to Exponential Technologies.

---

38 Peter H. Diamandis and Steven Kotler, *Abundance: The Future is Better Than You Think* (New York: Free Press, 2012).

39 "Disruptive Innovation: Why Now?" ARK Invest, last modified May 30, 2019, https://research.ark-invest.com/innovation-why-now.

QUESTIONS

1. What product or service your company makes is still dependent on physical components? How could it be digitized?

2. What is the digital technology that was supposed to transform your industry, but has not shown concrete results yet?

3. What expensive product or service would profoundly change the world if it became widely available and affordable?

4. What technological application reserved for researchers and fanatics is presently becoming available to less sophisticated users?

5. How would the lives and needs of your customers change if they had access to $1 million worth of the most advanced technology of today?

CHAPTER FIVE

VALUE FACILITATION

n 1996, I went to Boston to study English. While there, I
opened my first email account. I did so because I wanted
to be able to post my comments on the wall of the internet site of my favorite football team and the email was
required for the registration. It felt quite cool—that is,
until I realized that I didn't know anyone else with an
email account I could write to. The technology had very
limited value to me at the time. A few weeks later, my best
friend Filippo, who was also studying English in Boston,

opened his own account in order to register with the language school. Suddenly, I could email another person.

The value for the user of an email account is the ability to connect to someone else. Hence, if I have an email and no one else I know has it, it is absolutely worthless. After my best friend created his account, I now had a connection, which created immediate value.

A few weeks later, Filippo and I returned to Italy. Another friend opened his own email account when his family's business launched an internet site. Over the next school year, a dozen of my friends and acquaintances, for various reasons of their own, created email accounts. Every time they did so, the value of email *for me* grew.

There are two interesting facts to consider here. First, Filippo opened his account for his own reasons, completely independent of me. Even then, by doing so, he created value for me. The other fact is that when the next common friend joined, he created two connections—one between him and Filippo, and one with me. When another friend joined, he created three new connections and so on, with each new member creating increasing numbers of new connections and, therefore, value. This scales very rapidly as we discuss below. Just imagine, if a million users are present, adding a single new user creates one million new connections.

In economics, we call these two interesting facts externalities and network effects. An externality is a side effect of a decision made by someone else. They can be positive or negative. My friend's decision was a positive externality, because it created an advantage to me. This brings us to the network effect, according to which as the number of users grows, the value created increases exponentially. (See the Box on Metcalfe's Law for the logic behind this).

METCALFE'S LAW

Total number of connections =
{(Number of users − 1) x Number of users}/2

Every user connects to everybody else. So, the number of connections is number of users multiplied by the number of users. Of course, users don't connect to themselves (hence, the minus one in the formula). The total is divided by two because otherwise each connection would be counted twice.

When the number becomes large enough, the "minus one" becomes negligible and n x (n-1) becomes $n^2/2$, which is another exponential formula. So, the number of connections in a network grows exponentially as new users are added.

What this all means is that the number of connections in a network grows exponentially as the number of users grows. So the value of the network grows by adding new users, without a proportional increase in cost.

There are many businesses taking advantage of this phenomenon. Social media platforms, like Facebook, are an obvious example. Users are drawn by the presence of their family and friends, rather than just by the features of the platform. Google has tried for years to wrestle market share in this lucrative market. They launched Circles, then Google+.[1] Both folded.

Why? Couldn't Google launch a good social media platform?

Of course it could, and it arguably did. But it didn't matter. Users didn't care about the platform features. They cared about interacting with family and friends—and they were already on Facebook. This is not to suggest that only one social media platform can exist. More modestly, for the platforms whose main value proposition is connecting users, one platform will most likely dominate for given target audiences. Several platforms have been successful at attracting and coordinating specific users, depending on their purpose or demographics.

For example, LinkedIn is the leader in professional social networking. Twitter is for rapid communications. YouTube offers video capabilities. Instagram and Snapchat are especially popular with teenagers[2] and millennials. The Chinese platform TikTok/Douyin attracts a yet younger audience.[3] VK is the most popular social media platform for Russian speakers, as WeChat and Tencent QQ are for Chinese speakers.

1 Alex Hern, "Closure of Google : Everything You Need to Know," *The Guardian*, last modified February 1, 2019, https://www.theguardian.com/technology/2019/feb/01/closure-google-plus-everything-you-need-to-know.

2 Mark Sweney, "Is Facebook for Old People? Over-55s Flock in as the Young Leave," *The Guardian*, last modified February 12, 2018, https://www.theguardian.com/technology/2018/feb/12/is-facebook-for-old-people-over-55s-flock-in-as-the-young-leave.

3 Joshua Citarella, "Adventures in TikTok, the Wildly Popular Video App Where Gen Z Rules," *Artsy*, last modified December 3, 2018, https://www.artsy.net/article/artsy-editorial-tiktok-wildly-popular-video-app-gen-rules.

THE RISE OF THE PLATFORM BUSINESSES

These network externalities have massive consequences for the way companies operate and have opened the door for a profoundly different business model to come to the forefront. In their book *Platform Revolution*,[4] Geoffrey Parker, Marshall Van Alstyne, and Sangeet Choudary call traditional companies "pipeline" companies because their model works in that manner. In one end go the inputs—capital, human resources, raw materials, etc. The company works its magic, and out the other end of the pipe comes a service or product that is available to the market. Nearly all the costs to the company are at the entrance to the pipe, and all the revenue is at the exit. They traditionally succeed by achieving economies of scale, while defending themselves against competition. Most companies are built this way and use this type of production model, as shown in Figure 5a.

Now, we are seeing more and more platform businesses that operate completely differently from the traditional pipeline model. These businesses create the space for a network of users to interact with each other. You can see this in Figure 5b.

For example, Airbnb created a space where landlords can list their apartments for rent and tourists can rent them. When a tourist rents an apartment, he decides that using the

---

4   Geoffrey G. Parker, Marshall W. Van Alstyne, and Sangeet Paul Choudary, *Platform Revolution: How Networked Markets Are Transforming the Economy—And How to Make Them Work For You* (New York: W. W. Norton & Company, 2016).

landlord's property is worth more to him than the money. On the other hand, the landlord decides that the money is worth more to her than using the property. So, some value is created for both parties to the transaction. This is the core of any market exchange. Yet, Airbnb does not engage in any such transaction. It facilitates the value-creating transactions among users—hence the notion of Value Facilitation.

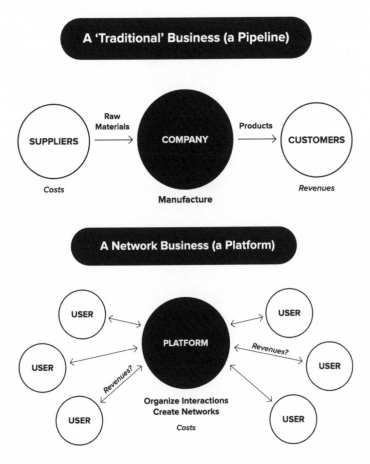

Figure 5a (top). Figure 5b (bottom).

This business model isn't new by any means. In *Matchmakers*, David Evans and Richard Schmalensee mention the examples of the emporion on Athens docks circa 300 BC and trade fairs in Renaissance Europe.[5] They existed to facilitate the exchanges between merchants, investors, and shipowners. A modern-day equivalent is a shopping mall. The only reason malls can rent out shopfronts for such exorbitant prices is because the operators of those storefronts know that shoppers go to the mall to shop because the experience of buying from multiple shops in one trip is made easier. Therefore, a mall's value is completely dependent on its ability to attract many shoppers and the right types of shops to make them more attractive to consumers.

That's a platform: a business model that creates value by facilitating relations and exchanges among a network of users. In other words, they exploit the externalities and network effects discussed above.

NETWORK EFFECTS

When more people join a platform, they create value for everybody else. It doesn't cost much for a company to add someone to a system, but it adds significant value. So, these effects can be extremely powerful. However, if the underlying network doesn't grow at the same speed, the addition of more users creates bottlenecks—a negative externality.

---

5   David S. Evans and Richard Schmalensee, *Matchmakers: The New Economics of Multisided Platforms* (Boston: Harvard Business Review Press, 2016).

The Bitcoin blockchain is a perfect example of what Value Facilitation looks like now. Bitcoin becomes more valuable when more people choose to use it. The more people that use it, the more businesses choose to accept it as a currency, and the easier it is for people to send and receive money. However, because of the way Bitcoin was designed, when too many people use it, the transactions become slow and backlogged. So, the more people that use Bitcoin, the more valuable it becomes, but the slower the service becomes.

Network effects can be direct or indirect. When someone joins a network, it creates more viable options for each current member, making the network more attractive. This, in turn, makes more people want to join. Again, Airbnb is a good example of such a dynamic.

Airbnb benefits from the pure direct effect, which states the more people there are on the network, the more attractive it becomes. The more tourists join, for example, the higher the chance for landlords to rent out their place. The more landlords join, the likelier that a tourist finds a desirable property. This is a reinforcing mechanism or a positive feedback loop.

Airbnb has also benefitted from some indirect network effects. When I lived in London in 2015, I had a beautiful apartment in Notting Hill. It was quite expensive, and I was planning to travel the entire summer. I thought I might try to rent it out on Airbnb, but there was one problem—it would require me to return to London to clean up after each guest and hand the keys off to the next guest. Obviously, this was not ideal.

Nowadays there are dozens of companies that solve this problem in the largest cities of the world by managing apartments on the platform on behalf of the landlords. For a fee, their agents do all the heavy lifting of posting photos, pricing, handing off keys, and cleaning up. This happens separately from the Airbnb website, and these companies are not directly affiliated with the platform.

Once Airbnb's network reached a certain size, it became interesting for agencies to make this type of service available. They, in turn, make Airbnb a more attractive service for would-be landlords. The complementary service indirectly increases the value of the network, drawing more users to the original platform.

TYPES OF PLATFORM BUSINESSES

Platform businesses can be classified based on how many different types of users transact on them. The simplest form is the one-sided platform. All users have similar expectations and preferences. For example, the value in a telephone is not in the telephone itself but in the interesting things that I say to the person I speak to or hear from. The value is in the connection with someone else. In most communication systems like the telephone, but also the fax machine, and later email, every user wants largely the same thing—effective, cheap, fast, quality communication.

Platforms become more interesting when they connect different types of users.

TWO-SIDED PLATFORMS

Two-sided platforms—those that involve two different kinds of users—have been very successful. Uber has riders and drivers. Airbnb has apartment owners and tourists. Facebook and Google connect advertisers with internet users. The business model of Apple's App Store also replicates this logic. The App Store makes it easy for a smartphone owner to buy software from an app developer, and in turn makes it easy for the app developer to sell it to the end user. What Apple does is make this connection easy—for a fee. Whenever you purchase an app, Apple takes a percentage of that fee. The more people use an iPhone, the more it becomes enticing for app developers to make their software available to that audience, and vice versa—the more apps that become available, the more interesting it is for consumers to own an iPhone.

The more you grow one side of the network, the more you create value for the other side.

Each of these users, however, has their own needs and expectations that sometimes conflict. Uber drivers want to have as many riders as possible in their network, because it gives them the opportunity to accept more rides. On the other hand, riders want to have as few active riders as possible, because that means there will always be a car available for them when they need one. Riders want to have as many drivers as possible to increase the likelihood of getting picked up quickly, while drivers want fewer drivers out there so there is less competition.

Managing a business of this type brings new issues and big decisions with it. Which side should the business prioritize?

What features can they develop to assist each side, and how will those features affect the evolution of the network? When you book an Uber, you tell the app where you are planning to go. However, Uber does not disclose this information to the driver until after they pick you up. Drivers would love to have this information because a short ride isn't going to be a high fare. They may consider such a trip a waste of time. However, a ride from the city center of London to Gatwick Airport is a very expensive ride that drivers would love to accept. If the driver had that knowledge, they may choose to skip certain riders in favor of others, which would ultimately damage the service. By not revealing that information, Uber is favoring its passengers over their drivers.

Another interesting feature in Uber's model is the ratings of passengers and drivers. If the rating of the driver gets too low, Uber blocks the app for the driver. Uber does this for the sake of passengers to ensure the quality of their experience. There are other apps that appear identical to Uber, except that the emphasis is predominantly on the drivers. One such company is called Careem.

Started in Dubai, Careem was designed to attract and retain drivers by creating stable employment and revenue for them. They focus heavily on training and giving them opportunities to have well-paid and respectable occupations in a region where being a driver is a low-paid, low-status profession. In wealthy countries like Saudi Arabia, Qatar, and the UAE, most drivers are foreigners from poorer countries. They don't have an attractive lifestyle and they're not very proud of their job. They perform their duties and send their money home, often living in fairly poor conditions.

One of the first things Careem did was call their drivers "Captains." This immediately changed their external and internal perception. By conversing with drivers who work for both Uber and Careem, I've listened time and again to anecdotes of how passengers from Careem are friendlier and more respectful to them.

Careem also provided Captains with excellent training with the mission of making their drivers into happy workers. They provide them with a stable income that is changing the trajectory of these individuals' lives. This is especially important in the countries where the Captains are locals, because it elevates their status within their social network and community.

So even two seemingly identical platform business models can specialize in providing a unique value proposition to one user type rather than the other.

MULTI-SIDED PLATFORMS

Some businesses have even more types of users—a dynamic that, of course, leads to more complications. For example, Microsoft Windows offers a platform for hardware makers, software developers, and users. YouTube has content creators, viewers, and advertisers. Advertisers want to have many content creators, many viewers, but few other advertisers. Viewers want to have no advertisers, many content creators, and may be indifferent to the number of viewers as long as they don't slow down the experience. Content creators want to have lots of advertisers, lots of viewers, and fewer content creators. YouTube must strike a balance somewhere to facilitate value creation in the meeting point between the users.

Alibaba manages multiple platforms, both B2B or B2C, targeted at Chinese or international users. Each platform can specialize to offer the features required by each pair of users, to support user growth and therefore accelerate direct network effects. Alibaba also launched a number of complementary services, like the payment service Alipay and the marketing service Alimama, to accelerate indirect network effects.

PLATFORM SECRETS

The value of a platform and its ability to compete ultimately depend on the size of its network. Hence, most of the platforms pursue a fast growth strategy (we'll discuss this in greater detail in chapter 8). Julian Birkinshaw[6] of London Business School calls this a 'turnstile logic' to protecting their business. The more users join a platform, the harder it is for competitors to challenge its business model.

Interestingly, as the network size increases, the cost of attracting new users does not. In fact, it may even *decrease*, as more potential users hear about the platform through

6   Julian Birkinshaw, "Ecosystem Businesses Are Changing the Rules of Strategy," *Harvard Business Review*, last modified August 8, 2019, https://hbr.org/2019/08/ecosystem-businesses-are-changing-the-rules-of-strategy.

word of mouth or are invited by existing users. This way, it is possible for platforms to grow in value relatively cheaply and incredibly fast.

For example, Jack Ma and his team launched the trading platform Alibaba in March 1999. By October, the platform had over forty thousand members—approximately half Chinese and half international. By December 2001,[7] they had reached one million users. Today, it has over 650 million users[8] and it aims to reach a whopping two billion users by 2036.[9] In the meantime, its payment system Alipay, launched in 2004, already has one billion users.[10]

Such speed is possible because networks don't need to build tangible industrial scale, as we discussed in chapter 1. Instead they coordinate existing, underused assets owned by users. This is strikingly evident in the case of Airbnb. Launched in 2008, it listed one million[11] properties by 2015. It now has over six million listings.[12] Traditional hotel operators, who need to develop physical properties, cannot

---

7   David S. Evans and Richard Schmalensee, *Matchmakers: The New Economics of Multisided Platforms* (Boston: Harvard Business Review Press, 2016).

8   Jon Russell and Rita Liao, "Alibaba Returns to Growth with Revenue up 51% to $13.9 Billion," TechCrunch, last modified May 15, 2019, https://techcrunch.com/2019/05/15/alibaba-2019-annual-earnings/.

9   Zhou Wenting, "Alibaba Aims for 2 Billion Users by 2036," China Daily, last modified December 19, 2018, http://global.chinadaily.com.cn/a/201812/19/WS5c1988f9a3107d4c3a001857.html.

10 https://intl.alipay.com/

11 Andrei Hagiu and Simon Rothman, "Network Effects Aren't Enough," *Harvard Business Review* (April 2016), accessed October 21, 2019, https://hbr.org/2016/04/network-effects-arent-enough.

12 "Fast Facts," Airbnb Newsroom, accessed October 21, 2019, https://news.airbnb.com/fast-facts/.

match such spectacular growth. For example, the largest hotel company in the world, Marriott, launched in 1957, took fifty-eight years to get to one million rooms and, even today, it has *only* 1.2 million rooms.[13] The second-largest hotel company, Hilton, launched one century ago, manages *only* 923,000 rooms.[14]

In fact, some platforms today have more users than most countries have citizens.[15] Instagram, WeChat, WhatsApp, and YouTube each have over one billion users. By comparison, the United States has 325 million citizens. At over two billion, Facebook users are *one-third of humanity*.

Because they leverage users who create value for each other, platforms employ fewer staff. For instance, Airbnb has just over three thousand employees. Hilton has 169,000 and Marriott 176,000. This lets them grow faster and achieve higher profitability.

These three core properties of platforms make them very successful business models. Among the ten most valuable global brands,[16] nine operate platforms. According to

---

13 Nancy Trejos, "The Brands and Hotel Rooms of Marriott International, by the Numbers," *USA Today*, last modified January 22, 2018, https://www.usatoday.com/story/travel/roadwarriorvoices/2018/01/22/brands-and-hotel-rooms-marriott-international-numbers/1053593001/.

14 https://www.hilton.com/en/corporate/

15 Jane C. Hu, "Social Networks Make the Worlds Largest Nations Seem Small," *Quartz*, last modified September 12, 2018, https://qz.com/1386649/social-networks-make-the-worlds-largest-nations-seem-small/.

16 "BrandZ Top 100 Most Valuable Global Brands 2018," WPP, last modified May 29, 2018, https://www.wpp.com/news/2018/05/brandz-top-100-most-valuable-global-brands-2018.

McKinsey,[17] seven of the world's twelve largest companies employ this model: Alibaba, Alphabet (the parent company of Google), Amazon, Apple, Facebook, Microsoft, and Tencent all operate platforms. The research also shows that by 2025 platforms will generate $60 trillion in revenue— that is more than 30 percent of global corporate revenue.

Platforms grow faster, with less capital and fewer employees, and achieve higher profitability than pipeline companies. So, how many established companies have adopted a platform strategy? Just 3 percent.[18]

ADAPTING YOUR BUSINESS IN THE AGE OF PLATFORMS

Given the increasing power of platforms, traditional pipeline businesses must make a strategic decision on how to respond.

The first option is to remain a pipeline that directly competes with the platform's value proposition. For example, some hotels are trying to compete with Airbnb by providing new services to consumers. Part of the appeal of Airbnb is the ability to connect with your host and forge a new social

---

17 Martin Hirt, "If You're Not Building an Ecosystem, Chances Are Your Competitors Are," McKinsey & Company, last modified June 12, 2018, https://www.mckinsey.com/business-functions/strategy-and-corporate-finance/our-insights/the-strategy-and-corporate-finance-blog/if-youre-not-building-an-ecosystem-chances-are-your-competitors-are.

18 Jacques Bughin and Nicolas van Zeebroeck, "New Evidence for the Power of Digital Platforms," *McKinsey Quarterly* (August 2017), accessed October 21, 2019, https://www.mckinsey.com/business-functions/digital-mckinsey/our-insights/new-evidence-for-the-power-of-digital-platforms.

connection in a foreign place. In response, many hotels are installing smaller bedrooms to make them cheaper, but also building comfortable external social areas, so tourists spend less time in the rooms and more time socializing with each other. Others organize concerts and events, offering tourists an authentic experience of the travel destination.[19] Yet others are installing kitchens[20] in the rooms and providing additional services, to make the travel experience more flexible.

The second option is to join existing platforms as a channel to provide their services. A newspaper may decide the best way to distribute their news is by way of Twitter, Facebook, and LinkedIn, because these platforms have changed the way their consumers behave. They must reach out to them through these channels because it's now necessary. Others distribute their goods via Alibaba or Amazon. In the hotel industry, bed and breakfasts and boutique hotels are making their rooms available through Airbnb.[21]

The third option is to become a platform company.

---

19 "How Hotels Are Competing with Airbnb," *The Daily Item*, last modified February 10, 2019, https://www.dailyitem.com/business/how-hotels-are-competing-with-airbnb/article_b50766ee-5ffb-5b2b-853b-13d5af60ade3.html.

20 Nikki Ekstein, "These New Hotels Can Actually Compete with Airbnb," *Bloomberg*, last modified July 26, 2018, https://www.bloomberg.com/news/articles/2018-07-26/these-new-hotels-can-actually-compete-with-airbnb.

21 "More Hotels Are Using Airbnb," Airbnb Newsroom, last modified January 16, 2019, https://press.airbnb.com/more-hotels-are-using-airbnb/.

TRANSITIONING COMPANIES

Pipeline companies embrace one of two main approaches to transition into platform companies.

The first is to innovate the business model to become a platform business. John Deere[22] has traditionally manufactured tractors and farming machinery. Now they have created a platform called MyJohnDeere, which connects all their farming vehicles through the internet on multiple servers. They collect data from the field and allow farmers to interact smoothly with different service providers. Based on the data collected by the tractor, the agronomist that's available through the platform can send instructions or make a recommendation. If a piece of machinery requires maintenance, a mechanic present on the platform is automatically informed.

Through the creation of a platform, John Deere is transforming into a service provider. At this point, they are no longer just selling tractors. Instead, they're offering farm management solutions. They do so by making farmers a part of their network to manage all the value creators in an accessible and easy way. Providers like crop experts, pest experts, seed providers, and weather providers all meet here to make the experience smoother, faster, and more value filled.

The second approach is to create a new platform. For example, Marriott is now launching its own property-rental

---

22 Cassie Perlman, "From Product to Platform: John Deere Revolutionizes Farming," Harvard Business School Digital Initiative, accessed October 21, 2019, https://digital.hbs.edu/data-and-analysis/product-platform-john-deere-revolutionizes-farming/.

platform to directly compete with Airbnb.[23] Marriott continues operating its pipeline business, while also operating a separate platform.

What remains one of the most famous examples is Amazon. It started as a pipeline business selling books to consumers. Then it opened to other merchants to the point where now external merchants can sell their goods through the Amazon platform. However, Amazon also keeps selling books, digital content, and many other everyday items under the Amazon Basics brand.[24] This is a pipeline business. They have shown that it is not only possible to transition from pipeline to platform, but also exist as a hybrid of the two.

Business models are not set in stone. They need to evolve as a company grows and external conditions change. LinkedIn initially started by making it possible for one type of user—professionals—to connect with each other and share their cvs online. It was a one-sided network. When enough of these users populated the network, the platform became interesting for recruiters and advertisers, among others, transitioning it into a multi-sided platform. A complementary service for these users is online training and education. So, LinkedIn acquired the online education platform Lynda and merged it into LinkedIn.

23 "Making Room for Airbnb," *The Wall Street Journal*, last modified May 20, 2019, https://www.wsj.com/articles/making-room-for-airbnb-11558394000.

24 Alvin Schwartz and Samuel Nocella, *Stores* (New York: MacMillan, 1977).

All user types on a network are not equal. Some create more value and are more critical to the success of the overall network. Other users are willing to pay to utilize a network so that they can access other users, while some are not. Facebook was initially only for private citizens or private users—or, more specifically, college students in certain colleges. Then, it opened to all users, and, like most media companies do when many people meet in one place, companies became interested in advertising on their platform. Today, companies are paying for the entire platform and subsidizing the general users, who access the services for free.

CULTIVATING ECOSYSTEMS

The skills, strategies, and mindset required to manage platforms are challenging for managers used to pursuing efficiency in pipelines. The vertical control over a company's resources is replaced by an open orchestration of external resources within an ecosystem of partners.

Ecosystems are large networks of customers, suppliers, producers, innovators, researchers, and regulators that collectively (and collaboratively, as in the case of Open Innovation discussed in chapter 2) create an outcome. For example, General Electric engages with one thousand entities in a value ecosystem that includes technology partners, system integrators, and software vendors. Sometimes customers improve on GE's systems faster than GE can.

Actors in an ecosystem play multiple roles at the same time. This can lead to quite unexpected outcomes. For example, Apple's iPhone/iOS platform competes with Google's Android platform for the dominance of smartphone apps. Yet, iPhone owners use Google's apps and services. So, these Google apps are critical for the success of Apple. At the same time Google pays Apple $12 billion[25] to remain the default search engine on Apple's browser Safari. Apple uses Google's cloud for its iCloud service.[26]

They are no longer only competitors; they are also each other's suppliers; they collaborate on industry standards.[27] They are co-opetitors. They compete as well as collaborate in the development and support of the global smartphone ecosystem. Interestingly, they are not very likely to put each other out of business, as competitors in the good old days attempted to do. To the contrary, in order to thrive, they need the other to thrive too.

QUESTIONS

1. What are the transactions your company engages in that create value for your customers? What is such value?

25 Lisa Marie Segarra, "Google to Pay Apple $12B to Remain Safaris Default Search: Report," *Fortune*, last modified September 29, 2018, https://fortune.com/2018/09/29/google-apple-safari-search-engine/.

26 Jordan Novet, "Apple Confirms It Uses Google's Cloud for iCloud," CNBC, last modified February 26, 2018, https://www.cnbc.com/2018/02/26/apple-confirms-it-uses-google-cloud-for-icloud.html.

27 Aaron Tilley, "Why Apple Joined Rivals Amazon, Google, Microsoft In AI Partnership," *Forbes*, last modified January 28, 2017, https://www.forbes.com/sites/aarontilley/2017/01/27/why-apple-joined-rivals-amazon-google-microsoft-in-ai-partnership/#680720665832.

2. What complementary services do other companies offer that add value to your offer? Could you provide them?

3. What are the main matchmakers (e.g., brokers, agents, or facilitators) in your industry? What are the main digital platforms in your industry, if any?

4. How do the matchmakers in your industry ensure that the right users are connected, and the most valuable exchanges are completed?

5. How could positive network effects unravel in your industry?

6. Would it be better for your company to compete with existing platforms, distribute through them, or establish a new platform?

CHAPTER SIX

ETHICAL CHAMPIONSHIP

Most companies that sell beauty products run campaigns with slim, conventionally attractive models who portray a standard of beauty that is both uniform and unattainable. Campaigns carry the implicit message that the consumer is nowhere near as good looking as the model. Their marketing technique is based on making the consumer feel inadequate and then selling them a fix. The larger consequence of this is that there are many women and girls who feel insecure or negative about their appearance. In fact, even the models themselves report feeling inadequate to the airbrushed "ideal."

In response to this, Unilever's beauty brand Dove decided to redevelop not just its ad campaigns, but the entire purpose of the brand. Instead of propping up these extreme and limiting perceptions of beauty, they redefined their messaging to communicate that their customers are already beautiful. They wanted to emphasize that a person's beauty comes from who they are, and that they don't need to pursue any standard of beauty but their own. Dove launched a campaign called "Real Beauty," in which they did not use professional models and instead hired women in a wide range of skin colors and body shapes. They put them all in an ad where they all wore white underwear to flaunt their bodies, stretch marks and all. Their message was that these women were real, and they were beautiful.

In 2013, Unilever also created several short films designed to go viral on social media and to generate a lot of engagement. One of these involved sketch artists that built portraits based on verbal descriptions. In this process, they asked the sketch artist to draw each woman's portrait using only her description of herself. Then, the artist drew another version of that same portrait based on someone else's description of her. When the portraits were compared, it became obvious which portraits were described by which person. The third party's descriptions always resulted in much more beautiful portraits because the women had poorer self-image compared to how others saw them. It showed how much more beautiful these women were than they perceived themselves, triggering a larger conversation about beauty standards in the media. Dove ran these communication campaigns because they wanted to change their philosophy as a company, opting to have a clear, positive, and meaningful impact on the world. This also resulted in an incredible engagement online and the image of the brand increased.

This is what Ethical Championship looks like. It's a company that creates strategic drivers to improve the world we live in.

UNETHICAL PRACTICES ARE BAD FOR BUSINESS

On the opposite end of the spectrum, we see how unethical behavior can devalue a brand.

In March 2018, it came to light that the consulting firm Cambridge Analytica had accessed the private records and information of about eighty-seven million Facebook users without their permission.[1] The CEO of Facebook, Mark Zuckerberg admitted this was a major breach of privacy.

This failure resulted in a 23 percent loss in market capitalization for Facebook in a matter of weeks, or over $120 billion.[2] To understand just how much money that is, they lost

---

1   Hanna Kozlowska, "The Cambridge Analytica Scandal Affected Nearly 40 Million More People than We Thought," Quartz, last modified April 4, 2018, https://qz.com/1245049/the-cambridge-analytica-scandal-affected-87-million-people-facebook-says/.

2   Sheera Frenkel, "Facebook Starts Paying a Price for Scandals," *The New York Times*, last modified July 25, 2018, http://www.nytimes.com/2018/07/25/technology/facebook-revenue-scandals.html.

more than the value of all of Nike ($110 billion) or Siemens ($112 billion) and just shy of the whole value of General Electric ($127 billion) or McDonald's ($130 billion).[3] You can't set money on fire that quickly.

One-fifth of Facebook's value was essentially wiped away. In this day and age, the fastest way to destroy value is arguably through an ethical scandal. This proves how massive the economic consequences of ethics are and how rapidly they play out. Even though Facebook picked back up a little, most analysts changed their target price of Facebook by lowering it by 10 percent. Steven Jay, a Swiss analyst, said the stock would be worth 10 percent lower in the long run because the company was no longer perceived to be low risk.

DRIVEN BY PURPOSE

In the past decade, many companies have embraced Corporate Social Responsibility (CSR). The most common way to achieve this is through the practice of philanthropy. The notion is that part of the reason that you are a successful business is that you operate in a context that makes it easier for you to succeed; where people are educated and there are infrastructures such that the whole community makes your success possible. Because the community has made this possible for you, it is essential that you give back. This idea

---

3   Erin Duffin, "Biggest Companies in the World 2019," Statista, last
     modified August 12, 2019, http://www.statista.com/statistics/263264/top-
     companies-in-the-world-by-market-value/.

of giving back is one of the major ways in which the trend of business ethics began.

While donating money to a museum or school is a benevolent act, it does not necessarily make your company "good." It can be far more relevant to look at the negative things your company has done and work to offset them. Some businesses, for example, calculate their environmental footprint and compensate by planting trees or taking other steps to reduce their negative impact. They don't necessarily actively try to do good, but they still look to improve their influence on the world by counterbalancing or removing the negative aspects of their business.

Purpose is more. The professional services EY Beacon[4] Institute and Harvard Business Review Analytics characterize purpose as "an aspirational reason for being which inspires and provides a call to action for an organization...and provides benefit to local and global society." Increasingly, we are seeing companies looking to achieve something meaningful—to go beyond just making money. Companies that are ethical champions are companies with this larger purpose—an overarching meaning involved in their pursuits beyond just making a profit. They also strive for more than giving back to society or minimizing their footprint. For example, Google's purpose is to organize the world's knowledge and make it easily accessible and available. Dove wants to change perceptions of real beauty.

---

4   "The Business Case for Purpose," *Harvard Business Review* (2015), accessed October 21, 2019, hbr.org/resources/pdfs/comm/ey/19392HBRReportEY.pdf.

Purpose can take many different shapes, the most traditional being simply to create value for shareholders. The trend of companies whose sole purpose is creating value for shareholders is dropping significantly in favor of the larger purpose of creating a positive impact on the world. Yet, there are many things one could do to make the world a better place.

What purpose should you pursue?

GENERATING PURPOSE

There is an unspoken global agreement that we must make the world a better place, because everybody wants to live in an increasingly better world. Our modern society has more resources in technology, wealth, and knowledge than ever before, yet large parts of the world are still dominated by hunger, conflict, and poverty.

We have an obligation to correct this imbalance and make the world a better place.

Amartya Sen, an economist, won the Nobel Peace Prize in 2001 because of a concept he developed that is still used by the United Nations and a number of other agencies. The idea is that the world becomes a better place when more people are able to do what they want, and they have a good reason to want it. We need to provide them with political freedom, a healthy environment, stable income, sufficient healthcare, and education so that they can make the best decisions for themselves. If one doesn't have enough money, they are not free, because our society requires that you earn a living. If one doesn't have their health, they are not free to pursue that which might make them happy. If they don't have an education, they might choose the wrong pursuits because they simply may not know any better. If a person spends their days inactive, drinking, and doing drugs, they are not expressing a measure of their freedom—they are doing it because they are ignorant of or do not have the economic opportunities to do something else.

To some extent, it is risky not to do so. There is an inherent danger in leaving billions of marginalized, poor, and uneducated people to fend for themselves. More importantly, they are human beings and deserve to be treated as such. They deserve to be given the opportunity to flourish.

In addition, many of our current environmental practices are unsustainable, meaning future generations might not be able to meet their own needs because we consume too many resources. We are already using the resources of three planets combined,[5] and the earth only can only absorb pollution, trash, and fossil fuels at a certain speed over the long term. This is a malevolent consumption of resources, and we don't have three planets to offset our use.

The UN has championed a broad global agreement to meet a set of seventeen Sustainable Development Goals[6] by the year 2030. These goals are ambitious and include ending

---

5   www.footprintnetwork.org
6   "About the Sustainable Development Goals - United Nations Sustainable Development," United Nations, accessed October 21, 2019, http://www.un.org/sustainabledevelopment/sustainable-development-goals/.

hunger and poverty, achieving gender equality, and achieving sustainable consumption of environmental resources. Deliberately and strategically pursuing any of these goals amounts to making the world a better place.

SUSTAINABLE DEVELOPMENT GOALS

In September 2015, the General Assembly of the United Nations (UN) adopted the resolution "Transforming our world: The 2030 Agenda for Sustainable Development" (United Nations 2015). The 2030 Agenda consists of a set of seventeen integrated Sustainable Development Goals, further divided into 169 individual targets. Ban Ki-moon,[7] Secretary-General of the UN at the time when the Agenda 2030 was launched, stressed the importance of the SDGs by declaring that they "are our shared vision of humanity and a social contract between the world's leaders and the people."

These are the SDGs:

Goal 1. End poverty in all its forms everywhere.
Goal 2. End hunger, achieve food security and improved nutrition, and promote sustainable agriculture.
Goal 3. Ensure healthy lives and promote well-being for all at all ages.
Goal 4. Ensure inclusive and equitable quality education and promote lifelong learning opportunities for all.

---

7 "United Nations Millennium Development Goals," United Nations, accessed October 21, 2019, https://www.un.org/millenniumgoals/.

Goal 5. Achieve gender equality and empower all women and girls.

Goal 6. Ensure availability and sustainable management of water and sanitation for all.

Goal 7. Ensure access to affordable, reliable, sustainable, and modern energy for all.

Goal 8. Promote sustained, inclusive, and sustainable economic growth, full and productive employment and decent work for all.

Goal 9. Build resilient infrastructure, promote inclusive and sustainable industrialization, and foster innovation.

Goal 10. Reduce inequality within and among countries.

Goal 11. Make cities and human settlements inclusive, safe, resilient, and sustainable.

Goal 12. Ensure sustainable consumption and production patterns.

Goal 13. Take urgent action to combat climate change and its impacts.

Goal 14. Conserve and sustainably use the oceans, seas, and marine resources for sustainable development.

Goal 15. Protect, restore, and promote sustainable use of terrestrial ecosystems, sustainably manage forests, combat desertification, and halt and reverse land degradation and halt biodiversity loss.

Goal 16. Promote peaceful and inclusive societies for sustainable development, provide access to justice for all and build effective, accountable, and inclusive institutions at all levels.

Goal 17. Strengthen the means of implementation and revitalize the global partnership for sustainable development.

While traditionally achieving these types of goals was considered the exclusive responsibility of governments, International Organizations, and NGOs, companies play—and must continue to play—a massive role in all of this. For a business to champion one of these goals would be a meaningful purpose, as it would represent an ethical driver to be weaved into their model and core strategies.

Isn't this too expensive? Can you afford it?

THE BUSINESS CASE FOR ETHICS

Businesses must be sustainable, first of all, from an economic point of view. They need to make enough money to keep doing what they do. They must also generate profits to reward risk and attract investors. These investments are critical for a business to be able to grow and succeed. In short, businesses need to make money. This is nonnegotiable. According to Professor Archie Carroll,[8] a trailblazer of CSR, it's their first and foremost responsibility.

To do so, they must use scarce resources efficiently and effectively—not wasting the world's resources to create

8 Archie B. Carroll, "The Pyramid of Corporate Social Responsibility: Toward the Moral Management of Organizational Stakeholders," *Business Horizons* 34, no. 4 (July 1991): 39–48, accessed October 21, 2019, https://www.sciencedirect.com/science/article/pii/000768139190005G.

value. Increasingly, the world is redefining what "value" means, how it is measured, and "value" for whom—meaning all stakeholders rather than just shareholders.

Yet, corporate responsibilities do not end with economic sustainability. Carroll says CSR also requires respecting the law—another nonnegotiable responsibility. Businesses that don't make money or that break the law have no license to operate. Once these conditions are met, two additional responsibilities become desirable: ethical and philanthropic. In other words, they need to behave ethically, according to what is expected of good members of society, and they can pursue philanthropic initiatives to do good.

Too many companies pay lip service to ethics. They strive to be profitable but consider the further responsibilities as burdens that reduce the bottom line. They don't grasp the connection between positive ethical purpose and value creation. The most successful businesses, instead, merge the four responsibilities into one overarching purpose.

Research has found that pursuing Ethical Championship can be quite beneficial to a business's bottom line. Ninety-seven percent[9] of executives of companies with purpose see a substantial long-term increase in the value of their company because of a strong positive impact on the world. Seventy-five percent see even short-term value gains. Furthermore, 73 percent of executives say that when they have a purpose or a drive for Ethical Championship integrated into business

---

9   "Newsroom," EY, accessed October 21, 2019, http://www.ey.com/gl/
    en/newsroom/news-releases/news-ey-purpose-not-profit-is-business-
    leaders-key-to-success-amid-turbulent-global-economy.

operations, it becomes easier to navigate because it gives a company direction. Strategic decision making, innovation, and change become easier. In short, purpose creates a distinct competitive advantage which drives performance and profitability.

The most evident example is that companies benefit from the extra reach of customers and revenues through Ethical Championship because these positive impact brands are preferred by consumers. Market research company Nielsen reports that customers, across generations and geography, increasingly demand sustainable[10] companies. These are not mere statements. Nielsen also reports that sales[11] of sustainable products dwarf those of traditional products.

The Real Beauty campaign of Dove, for example, impacted the bottom line. After launch, sales went up 700 percent in just six months.[12] Unilever is a multinational consumer goods company, with a portfolio of over four hundred brands. Among these brands, a dozen are worth over $1 billion—household names like Axe, Knorr, Lipton, and Magnum. Today, Dove is Unilever's biggest brand.[13]

---

10 "Global Consumers Seek Companies That Care About Environmental Issues," *Nielsen*, last modified September 11, 2018, https://www.nielsen.com/eu/en/insights/article/2018/global-consumers-seek-companies-that-care-about-environmental-issues.

11 "What's Sustainability Got To Do With It?" *Nielsen*, last modified October 16, 2018, https://www.nielsen.com/us/en/insights/report/2018/whats-sustainability-got-to-do-with-it/.

12 Stephen Brook, "'Real Women' Ads Do Wonders for Dove Figures," *The Guardian*, last modified July 29, 2004, http://www.theguardian.com/media/2004/jul/29/marketingandpr.advertising1.

13 "Unilever's Sustainable Living Plan Continues to Fuel Growth," Unilever, last modified October 5, 2018, http://www.unilever.com/...

The success of Dove was such that Unilever kept investing in brands with purpose, which it calls "sustainable living brands." In 2015, they had twelve of them. In 2016, they increased that number to eighteen. In 2017, out of their top forty performing brands, twenty-two of them focused on sustainable living initiatives associated with positive ethical issues. Furthermore, these sustainable living brands grew 46 percent faster than all their other brands and accounted for 70 percent of the company's revenue growth.

Unfortunately, there are no shortcuts to achieve these results.

YOU MUST PRACTICE WHAT YOU PREACH

To get credit for pursuing a positive social impact, you must be credibly ethical yourself, on both a business and personal level. You can't tell your employees not to cheat and lie while you are cheating on your taxes and spouse in your personal life. To be credible and to have a trustworthy message, you need to behave like an ethical person. Likewise, to benefit from corporate Ethical Championship, businesses themselves need to become ethical.

This means that company culture needs to be respectful towards all internal and external stakeholders, that is anyone who has an interest in the operations of the company. Internal stakeholders are employees and shareholders, and

---

...news/press-releases/2018/unilevers-sustainable-living-plan-continues-to-fuel-growth.html.

external stakeholders are customers, the government, the environment, and society. Being respectful of all of them is a pre-condition to credibly pursuing Ethical Championship.

British Petroleum, now BP, is one of the most high-profile examples of *not* walking the talk. The company invested a significant amount of money to change its image through a major rebranding effort, going from British Petroleum to Beyond Petroleum. They created a new logo with the familiar yellow and green sun.

Then disaster struck.

BP was running a critical Deepwater Horizon rig in the Gulf of Mexico, and they employed less than adequate safety standards. On April 10, 2010, there was an explosion that killed eleven people. The rig sank while oil was still rushing out of it, causing an enormous oil spill, one that is considered the greatest environmental disaster in US history. This tragedy hurt BP, as it lost 55 percent[14] of its value on the stock market and BP's image was destroyed. The overall cost of cleaning up and settling the core lawsuits surrounding this event has cost the company $65 billion.[15] The stock did eventually recover a little bit, but it never achieved its initial glory.

----

14 Alex Chamberlin, "BP Lost 55% Shareholder Value after the Deepwater Horizon Incident," Market Realist, last modified September 10, 2014, https://marketrealist.com/2014/09/bp-lost-55-shareholder-value-deepwater-horizon-incident/.

15 Ron Bousso, "BP Deepwater Horizon Costs Balloon to $65 Billion," *Reuters*, last modified January 16, 2018, http://www.reuters.com/article/us-bp-deepwaterhorizon/bp-deepwater-horizon-costs-balloon-to-65-billion-idUSKBN1F50NL.

The accident revealed that everything they tried to promote through their rebranding did not correspond to any of their deeper values. While spending money on their image, they were saving money on maintenance of the rig, creating a huge risk for the employees and the impact on the environment. The losses they suffered were far more than just financial, and the world itself suffered as well.

Given the chance to hire a manager who worked at BP at the time and was responsible for the decision that cost his employer $65 billion, most wouldn't. Irrespective of any ethical judgment, they would consider him simply a poor manager.

SUSTAINABILITY AND RISK

Operating unethically or unsustainably is poor management. It carries risks that can affect the business models of almost every kind of corporation. Tensie Whelan, the director of the Center for Sustainable Business at NYU Stern School of Business, and Carly Fink of the Rainforest Alliance assembled an impressive set of data[16] that make a strong case for sustainable business practices. They report that 72 percent of suppliers to large national operations in developing countries believe their business models are threatened by global warming and other types of environmental risks.

---

16 Tensie Whelan and Carly Fink, "The Comprehensive Business Case for Sustainability," *Harvard Business Review*, last modified October 21, 2016, https://hbr.org/2016/10/the-comprehensive-business-case-for-sustainability.

Bunge, a leading producer of sugar and ethanol in Brazil, lost $60 million in operation costs biofuel because of a 2010 drought. Floods in 2011 damaged several companies in Southeast Asia that manufactured textiles for western retailers. The same is happening for producers of coffee, chocolate, and other raw materials particularly sensitive to climate change. Unfortunately, many of those businesses are in emerging economies and have difficulty absorbing large financial hits.

Another benefit of Ethical Championship is that by reducing environmental impact, companies generally increase efficiency. Using renewable energies, consuming less fuel, or simply creating and manufacturing in a way that creates less waste automatically translates to lower costs. For example, Unilever estimates cumulative energy savings of $678 million in ten years. Many other companies are embracing an integrated approach to decouple their economic performance from the extractions and consumption of natural resources. This approach, called circular economy,[17] consists of designing products in such a way that they can be recycled more efficiently, so that the last stage in the life cycle of a product is also the first stage in the life cycle of a new product. For example, the computer maker Dell[18] uses

---

17 Terence Tse, Mark Esposito, and Khaled Soufani, "How Businesses Can Support a Circular Economy," *Harvard Business Review*, last modified February 1, 2016, https://hbr.org/2016/02/how-businesses-can-support-a-circular-economy.

18 "Sustainable Products and Services," Dell, accessed October 21, 2019, https://www.dell.com/learn/us/en/uscorp1/corp-comm/closed-loop-recycled-content.

plastic from old computers to manufacture new ones, capital goods maker Caterpillar[19] restores old machinery to new life, and energy management company Schneider Electric[20] is recycling its packing materials. These efforts reduce the environmental footprint of economic activity—and costs.

ETHICS DRIVES INNOVATION...

Ethical champions look for novel ways of doing things. Pursuing social impact very often means motivating a company to innovate. When Unilever analyzed the company's energy consumption and environmental impact, they realized a significant part of the energy consumption associated with their brand came from the way customers consume their products. For example, a large part of a washing machine's energy consumption comes from using hot water. As a result, they developed soaps that could be used in cold washes, reducing the amount of energy consumers use to wash their clothes.

There are desperate water shortages in South Africa. To combat this, Proctor and Gamble developed soap for handwashing that requires less rinsing and thus less water. They saw an opportunity to sell a product as well as a chance to help solve an environmental quandary. These innovations

---

19 "Circular Economy," Caterpillar, accessed OCtober 21, 2019, https://www.caterpillar.com/en/company/sustainability/remanufacturing.html.

20 "Circular Economy Commitments," Schneider Electric, accessed October 21, 2019, https://www.schneider-electric.com/en/about-us/press/news/corporate-2018/circular-economy-commitments.jsp.

reduce impact on the environment, and it benefits the user as well.

The World Economic Forum issues an annual global report wherein they interview hundreds of CEOs in the largest companies in the world. They are asked to assess the greatest threats and risks to businesses for the near future and classify them according to how likely they are to occur and how impactful they will be. The 2019 report[21] revealed that five of the top six risks and each of the top three are related to the environment—extreme weather events, failure to mitigate climate change, and other natural disasters. All are considered to be extremely likely and dramatically impactful.

Companies like Unilever, Procter and Gamble, and other ethical champions must continue to find ways to actively oppose these threats to our environment, simultaneously creating value while helping to save our planet.

...AND FACILITATES CHANGE

When you strive to have an overarching positive impact on society, transformative and organizational change become easier. Typically, employees are resistant to institutional change, but when the specific changes are driven by goals to improve the greater good, it's much easier to communicate the meaning and reason behind the changes. It's easier

---

21 "The Global Risks Report 2019," World Economic Forum, last modified January 15, 2019, https://www.weforum.org/reports/the-global-risks-report-2019.

for employees to get on board, because they believe in the causes you are supporting. This belief in and behavior of a company being an ethical champion brings with it better, more motivated, and more loyal employees. Quality workers want to work for companies that do good.

Conversely, quite a few Google[22] employees resigned when Google began collaborating with the US government on unmanned drones for use in intelligence operations. For organizations in this digital era—this new industrial revolution where physical manufacturing and scale are no longer competitive advantages—the advantage comes from software and services. This is a knowledge economy in which the main assets are data and people. If decisions you make send your best people away, that becomes a value-destroying decision. If your decisions help attract, motivate, and engage employees, that's a value-creating decision. It is obvious that the latter is what a business leader should do.

THE BOTTOM LINE ON ETHICAL CHAMPIONSHIP

Pivoting your company's mission towards improving the world can be an extremely powerful way to unite and energize your organization. It can improve your company's image and potentially boost profits. In fact, research by author Raj Sisodia, for the second edition of his bestseller

---

22 Kate Conger, "Google Employees Resign in Protest Against Pentagon Contract," Gizmodo, last modified May 14, 2018, https://gizmodo.com/ google-employees-resign-in-protest-against-pentagon-con-1825729300.

Firms of Endearment, found that companies that operate with a clear and driving sense of purpose, beyond the goal of just making money, outperformed the S&P 500 by a factor of fourteen between 1998 and 2013

To do good, however, you must also be good. Hollow activism is easy to spot and easily turns off potential customers, employees, and shareholders. You must truly commit to the principles that you espouse by being an ethical organization and working to make the world a better place. Furthermore, achieving these sustainable development goals reduces the greatest threat to businesses of all, which is the market and society's stability. Businesses cannot be run profitably in unstable markets and societies. Sustainable development goals substantially reduce this risk.

From a larger societal perspective, it's important that businesses align with ethical issues due to the way we surround ourselves with products and messages. The world's five hundred largest companies have revenues equivalent to 38 percent of the world's GDP.[23] Unilever's products are used in private homes around the world and touch the lives of 2.5 billion people, far beyond the reach of any government. The business's unparalleled reach gives them a huge platform to spread ethical ideas and sustainable habits.

With all of these global considerations, we must keep in mind always that the world is changing around us at a rapid rate. The final "R" of CLEVER relates to the Responsive

---

23   Christopher Tkaczyk, Stacy Jones, and Grace Donnelly, "The Global 500 Explained in 6 Easy Charts," *Fortune,* last modified August 8, 2017, https://fortune.com/2016/07/22/global-500-in-6-charts/.

Decision Making required to determine whether what you're doing is still effective when those changes occur. We'll explore that concept in chapter 7.

QUESTIONS

1. What can your company do to make the world a better place?
2. If your company did not exist, would the world require that it be created just the way it is now?
3. Are savings possible by repurposing or recycling your old products into new ones?
4. Would you be able to develop a product to serve the poorest people on the planet?
5. Is there anything your company does that would make you ashamed if it was published on the local news?
6. Do you ever make decisions that might compromise the survival of your company?
7. Would you be okay with being considered a poor manager?

CHAPTER 7

RESPONSIVE DECISION MAKING

W hen I worked at the American University of Beirut, one of the foremost educational institutions in the Middle East, I met with many businessmen and entrepreneurs from the region. During one such meeting I remember discussing strategy with an entrepreneur. He told me that whenever he realized he was planning anything beyond six months into the future, he killed the plan and went back to the drawing board until he had a new shorter plan. He recognized that

Lebanon was an unstable country and that in such a context, long-term plans do not work. To this day I find that observation very insightful and valuable.

That's not to say that if your business is located in Switzerland, you should approach planning in exactly the same way. There are obviously more stable contexts and industries, where some degree of long-term planning is possible and even advisable—but even there, you must develop the ability to react quickly, because—we've said it before, and it bears repeating—the world is increasingly VUCA.

When conditions change, the critical issue from a business perspective is that you no longer know whether something you were sure of is still true. Think about some of the examples we've discussed. Companies no longer operate within an industry, machines learn faster than people, competitors need each other to succeed, success requires that you fail more. When you don't know for sure anymore, you must be willing to unlearn the things you used to believe in and quick to learn the new truths. Many companies continue on in their same manner of doing business because it's what has made them successful in the past. So, they operate under the tacit assumption that nothing is going to change or that change will not affect them. In a VUCA environment, that assumption is guaranteed to be mistaken. You must take a different approach.

Responsive Decision Making is the principle of continuous and deliberate learning that allows you to make decisions in response to what you've learned, and not based on outdated wisdom, wishful assumptions, or leaps of faith.

From a practical perspective, many companies have a five-year and ten-year strategy. However, the things we believed five years ago about today were quite naïve. We can't be faulted for it—we're human. We tend to project what we see now into the future and don't anticipate as much change as we will actually experience. That means that in addition to having these strategic plans, you also need to learn how to make faster and more reactive decisions of a strategic nature. After a conference, a manager approached me to confess that her company still puts much effort into their five-year plan. In fact, they put so much effort into it that they create a new five-year plan, *each and every year*. It may sound funny, but that's the right approach! Companies need to plan for the future. They should not, however, stick to these plans until the future comes.

One company that deeply embeds this into its spirit is Amazon. In a letter to the shareholders, CEO Jeff Bezos wrote that everyone must go to work each day as if it were day one,[1] because day one is when you don't know anything yet. You don't have a consolidated way of working. You're constantly trying to do things right for the first time. You're learning and testing. There is an attitude of discovery, and Bezos wanted that attitude to be present in the business on a daily basis.

What if you don't? What if you stick to a long-term plan based on assumptions?

---

1   Justin Bariso, "This Original Letter From Jeff Bezos to Amazon Shareholders Teaches Some Extraordinary Lessons in Leadership," Inc., last modified April 20, 2017, https://www.inc.com/justin-bariso/20-years-ago-amazons-jeff-bezos-sent-an-extraordinary-letter-to-shareholders.html.

SEGWAY

Segway, the two-wheeled personal vehicle, was supposed to revolutionize transportation. It was developed in secret over a decade,[2] and it was finally released with significant fanfare with a televised launch.

It was an almost immediate dud.

After all the hype, people didn't find the technology particularly useful. Segways were expensive, slow, and the average person saw no need for them.[3] Set to manufacture—and sell—ten thousand units per week, it managed to sell ten thousand in two years.[4]

Within the first five years, the company only sold thirty thousand units. Considering they spent $100 million[5] developing the product, that was an enormous flop. The leaders of the company saw this piece of machinery as a great bit of futuristic technology, but they failed in their understanding of what customers really needed or wanted. They made a product, but they did not address a need. While the

2   Nicole Perlroth, "Dean Kamen's Legacy Project," *Forbes*, last modified July 16, 2012, https://www.forbes.com/forbes/2009/0824/thought-leaders-segway-dean-kamen-legacy-project.html#469147b4692e.

3   Robert Klara, "Remember the Segway? Here's Why It Never Quite Took Off," *Adweek*, last modified January 4, 2016, https://www.adweek.com/brand-marketing/remember-segway-heres-why-it-never-quite-took-168789/.

4   Nina Sovich, "Segway Slump," CNN Money, last modified April 1, 2004, https://money.cnn.com/magazines/fsb/fsb_archive/2004/04/01/366638/index.htm.

5   Jordan Golson, "Well, That Didnt Work: The Segway Is a Technological Marvel. Too Bad It Doesnt Make Any Sense," *Wired*, last modified January 16, 2015, https://www.wired.com/2015/01/well-didnt-work-segway-technological-marvel-bad-doesnt-make-sense/.

company eventually bounced back, and now serves several niches like security officers at airports, its intended plan to revolutionize the way the world walks did not materialize.

Segway would have been better off actively exploring, testing, and learning what the potential customers thought of the product.

RENT THE RUNWAY

Contrast Segway to Rent the Runway. They make it possible to live without owning clothes. Instead, customers can sign up for a subscription to continuously rent clothes, without buying them. This sounds more far-fetched than the Segway.

How did they launch?

In their basic service, you can rent designer clothes which are very expensive, and which are also worn quite rarely. For example, a woman might purchase an evening gown worth $3,000 and then use it only a couple of times in her life, on special occasions and ceremonies. Instead of spending such exorbitant amounts of money on infrequently worn items, Rent the Runway offers consumers the chance to rent these high-ticket items.

Before buying all of the expensive designer clothes they needed in order to have product to rent, and before securing a facility and a warehouse, they chose to test the market to see if there was a demand. They set up a series of "trunk shows" where they invited potential customers to a space where they offered designer dresses for rent. The response was very positive.

So, did they launch? Not yet.

There were many other factors to consider. The founders knew that if they only offered the service online, their customers would not be able to touch and try on the clothes as they had in the trunk show. So, they held a second one where the customers were only allowed to see the clothes but not try them on. Once again, the response was positive.

Did they launch now? Not yet.

The founders also realized that an online rental experience removed the social element where customers could bring their friends to get their opinions and enjoy the shopping experience together. To test whether this would be a factor, they sent a PDF via email to their mailing list that contained photos of the clothes. Five percent of the women on this mailing list were still willing to rent a dress without seeing it, touching it, trying it on, or discussing it with others.

Five percent might seem small, but they considered it okay. They recognized that not everyone had to be or would be their customer. So, they launched.

Rent the Runway is now a thriving business. It has achieved the coveted "unicorn" status—or a valuation of $1 billion.[6] Yet, before launch, it was a concept built on a set of uncertainties. Women will rent a designer dress online: True or false? They will rent without trying it on: True or false? They will return the dress on time and in good conditions: True or false?

---

6   Megan Rose Dickey, "Rent the Runway Hits a $1 Billion Valuation," TechCrunch, last modified March 21, 2019, https://techcrunch.com/2019/03/21/rent-the-runway-hits-a-1-billion-valuation/.

The founders hoped so. They also accepted that they did not know the answers to these questions. Instead, each element of their business model was just a hypothesis that could be true or false. So, they took their concept and tested it extensively, rapidly, and cheaply. Doing so helped them learn what was true and what wasn't, what worked and what didn't. When Rent the Runway finally launched, most uncertainties had already been tested and confirmed. This saved them time, money, and effort. It also ensured that they would not fail.

They even learnt that some customers are willing to pay a monthly subscription and access an almost unlimited closet, which liberates them from ever buying clothes again.

THINKING LEAN

Rent the Runway is a great example of a "lean startup."[7] The concept of lean came from the manufacturing world, and it is centered on the idea of minimizing waste. It emphasizes learning what you don't know for sure as rapidly and as efficiently as possible. Prior to lean thinking, companies imagined a business plan that worked according to their assumptions of what customers want, what they'd be willing to pay, and what would be the revenues. That's what Segway had done. For example, in their business plan, they expected to rake in $12 billion in sales in their first year. However,

---

7   Eric Ries, *The Lean Startup: How Today's Entrepreneurs Use Continuous Innovation to Create Radically Successful Businesses* (New York: Crown Business, 2011).

because these were only assumptions, they would build and launch the new products based on no actual knowledge and then found out there was no one there to buy it.

Lean thinking is a methodology that fast tracks learning. Instead of building a product and then trying to sell it, would-be entrepreneurs define their business idea and selectively test their assumptions, then make improvements. Companies do this by developing an MVP, or minimally viable product, which captures the essence of their idea. This means it's not the best product you can develop, but one that meets the minimal requirements for you to get the necessary feedback from your customers. This is not your fully developed Segway; it's your rough and imperfect trunk show. Then, consumers interact with it to either confirm or debunk the utility of the product, and you can iterate on it as necessary.

Dropbox is an excellent example of this mode of thinking. Before writing all the sophisticated code required for its service to work, the creators wanted to make sure people were actually willing to use it. One MVP of Dropbox was a simple video that showed an example of how the system would work in the future once the technology had been developed. When the response to the video was overwhelmingly positive, the developers decided to proceed with their product because they knew there would be demand for it.

Sometimes after testing, the results may show that a model doesn't work. At this point, the developer should either improve on it or drop it for good. To improve it, they continue testing it over and over.

The Lean approach helps companies test if a business model works, without making huge initial investments. This new way of thinking stimulates a new way of looking at problem-solving and innovation as a process of continuous learning.

It is easy to embrace this approach as a startup with nothing to lose. Established companies, too, stand to benefit from this learning approach.

AN ADVENTURE IN HEALTHCARE

Doug Dietz was the architect behind General Electric's GE Healthcare brand. They developed and designed CT scans, MRI machines, and other medical imaging devices. GE leased out these very expensive and advanced machines to hospitals and clinics. These machines are designed by experienced professionals, with great technical knowledge and expertise.

Mr. Dietz[8] went to a hospital to observe his machines in action and, for the first time, saw how they were working for patients and medical operators. Unfortunately, these machines were a source of very unpleasant experiences, particularly for children. He saw scared, crying, and desperate children with their parents trying to console them as they went through these cramped and noisy machines. He

---

8 "From Terrifying to Terrific: The Creative Journey of the Adventure Series," GE, last modified September 20, 2012, http://newsroom. gehealthcare.com/from-terrifying-to-terrific-creative-journey-of-the-adventure-series/.

found out that 80 percent[9] of children needed to be sedated for medical imaging, which in addition to being expensive, added risks for the patients.

Surely, there was room for improvement.

In response to this realization, GE decided to adapt their product by changing the look of the rooms in which these machines were installed. They named the project Adventure Series and created a whole storytelling experience around the machines. Some of the machines were decorated with tropical colors, for example, and designed with such themes as "pirate adventure." When the child needed to lay still, the experience was framed as the child needing to remain motionless so an evil pirate wouldn't see them. In terms of noise, the pirate angle framed noises as cannon shots. In another experience, the children were on a canoe and had to stay still so as not to rock the boat. They even projected the image of a fish jumping over the canoe, so the child knew to stay low.

GE managed to transform the experiences of many children, with the overarching effect that less than 1 percent of kids who used their newly updated technology needed to be sedated. In fact, one child asked her parents if she could come back to do it again the following day. This came from a better understanding of the experience and the context of its use from the user's perspective.

9   Evan Porter, "Kids at This Hospital Were Terrified of the Machines— Until They Got a Makeover," Upworthy, last modified November 8, 2017, https://www.upworthy.com/kids-at-this-hospital-were-terrified-of-the-machines-until-they-got-a-makeover.

How can you improve your understanding of users and context and find better solutions to their problems?

DESIGN THINKING

An increasingly popular and successful methodology is design thinking, championed by creative company IDEO[10] and brought to business mainstream by thought leaders such as Jeanne Liedtka[11] and Roger Martin.[12] Design thinking achieved transformed problem-solving, particularly when the problem is ill specified and solutions uncertain, from an exercise in guesswork to a structured process.

This is how it works.

EMPATHIZE: UNDERSTANDING THE USER

There's a famous saying by Professor Theodore Levitt[13] of Harvard Business School that, "people don't want to buy a quarter-inch drill. They want a quarter-inch hole!" This is true of most goods and services, with very few exceptions. People buy most products as a means to an end. When

10 Tim Brown, "Design Thinking," *Harvard Business Review* (June 2008), accessed October 21, 2019, https://hbr.org/2008/06/design-thinking.

11 Jeanne Liedtka, "Why Design Thinking Works," *Harvard Business Review* (September-October 2018), accessed October 21, 2019, https://hbr.org/2018/09/why-design-thinking-works.

12 "Rotman on Design: The Best on Design Thinking from Rotman Magazine," Rotman, accessed October 21, 2019, http://www.rotman.utoronto.ca/Connect/Rotman-MAG/Rotman-On-Design-Book.

13 Clayton M. Christensen, Scott Cook, and Taddy Hall, "What Customers Want from Your Products," Harvard Business School, last modified January 16, 2006, https://hbswk.hbs.edu/item/what-customers-want-from-your-products.

making decisions, it's important to understand what that end is. You didn't buy CLEVER because you wanted a book. My clients don't hire me because they like to hear my voice. My students don't take my courses because they enjoy coming to class. They want to succeed in their careers. They read CLEVER and listen to me because this will make them successful. If they find a better way to achieve their goal, CLEVER will disappear, no matter how much new content I add.

Professor Clayton Christensen[14] calls this concept the "job to be done."

To understand what a customer wants to achieve, it's essential to acknowledge the problem the customer is trying to solve, as well as to note the circumstances or context surrounding the problem. Empathize by defining the user's point of view and identifying the problem. Understanding the context of the user helps zoom in on the solution needed to deliver.

DEFINE THE PROBLEM

Defining a problem is just as it sounds—making a clear statement of exactly what issue you are going to solve. You can describe it with the following structure—user X has problem Y in the context of Z. This stage is very important, because often the problem is not what it appears to be.

---

14 Clayton M. Christensen, Taddy Hall, Karen Dillon, and David S. Duncan, "Know Your Customers' 'Jobs to Be Done,'" *Harvard Business Review* (September 2016), accessed October 21, 2019, https://hbr.org/2016/09/ know-your-customers-jobs-to-be-done.

Consider, for example, the evolution of the elevator. Waiting for the elevator in tall buildings such as skyscrapers became a frustrating experience, making people quite unhappy. There were many solutions to this problem, including manufacturing larger elevators. Larger elevators, however, were more expensive, cumbersome, and needed larger engines. Another solution was to make elevators very fast—a tactic that was also potentially more expensive, required more maintenance, or could have made riders sick from the speed.

The solution that's now employed around the world is mirrors installed near and inside all elevators. This solution doesn't make the wait or trip time any shorter, but riders aren't as bored anymore because they are busy looking at themselves—funny but true. The problem was not really the waiting time. It was the *perception* of the waiting time. This simple but effective tactic reduces the perception of waiting time. It's a successful solution because it's inexpensive and comes from understanding the problem of the user and the context.

IDEATE

After defining a problem and the perspective of the user, the next step is coming up with an idea to solve the problem. Ideation requires multiple creative thinking techniques and consists of generating multiple possible and practical solutions. This may include reframing or redefining the problem to look at it in a different way. The key is not settling with your first idea. Your first idea will be—in most circumstances—the most intuitive and so also the most obvious. That usually won't do.

You want an exceptional idea.

Unfortunately, most of your ideas are not exceptional. On average, your ideas are, well, *average*. So, you want many of them.

Wait, what?

Since we don't know for sure how to generate an exceptional idea, we want to generate as many as possible, in order to increase the chances of generating an exceptionally good one. The quality of ideas follows a normal, or Gaussian, distribution. Normal distributions are bell-shaped. The largest number of observations are average, and the further away you move from the average the fewer cases are observed. For ideas, exceptionally good ideas are very rare, so are exceptionally bad ones. Most ideas are average or around average. Figure 6 illustrates this point. The full line represents the distribution of the quality of different ideas.

The large majority of ideas, including good ones, won't be good enough, but that doesn't matter, as long as there is at least one exceptionally good idea. The little grey area at the end of the distribution represents the chances that a new idea is exceptionally good. It's a very small chance, but it can be improved.

The dashed line shows that you can increase the chances of generating an exceptional idea by simply generating more ideas. Another way to do so is to increase the variety of ideas. The dotted line shows what just happens. The ideas will be *worse*, on average. Yet, there is a higher chance of striking gold.

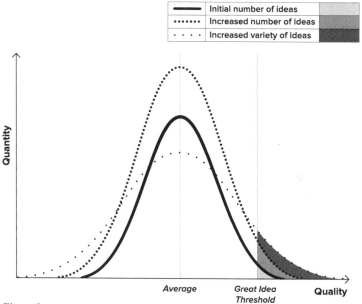

| Initial number of ideas |
| Increased number of ideas |
| Increased variety of ideas |

Figure 6.

The World Economic Forum invites stakeholders from corporations, academia, government, and civil society to its workshops, to facilitate this type of cross fertilization (another form of Collaborative Intelligence, as we mentioned in chapter 2). Many companies I work with run hackathons and other initiatives, where we sometimes invite external participants, precisely with this goal. At Hult International Business School, I've co-developed and ran for a few years a pre-university program, where high school students ideated new products for companies such as Ford Motors, Electronic Arts, and Unilever. Many of the ideas we generate at these events are still green, some are hard to implement, some are not even very creative—but there are invariably a handful of pure gems that justify the effort.

PROTOTYPE

Once there are multiple solutions on the table, it's essential to know which work and which don't. So, we need to test them. Yet, instead of developing them completely, we build prototypes. Prototypes are a simpler, cheaper version of the possible solutions. We use it to gauge consumers' responses for further refinement before launch.

The original Segway was quite expensive, it needed eight hours to recharge, and only had a range of twenty-five to thirty kilometers. Also, most consumers found riding it unnatural and unsafe. If consumers didn't like these features or felt the product was too expensive, a prototype might have helped identify these issues early on and allowed them, as we'll cover next, to course correct as needed.

TEST

The way users interact and use a prototype provides very valuable information. It also provides ideas on how to improve or fix an idea.

As an example, consider the sugar packet. Traditionally, a sugar packet is a rectangle that you pick up, shake, tear the corner with your fingers, and pour. Four simple steps.

Then a designer came along with sugar packets in the shape of a long tube. The concept was such that you could hold the packet with your first three fingers and push with your thumb through the paper, and with one gesture, would break through the paper and the sugar would come down. It's a greatly improved version of the traditional sugar packet.

The problem was that no one had enough of a problem with the traditional version—there was no consumer need for the new design. It was also unclear to the user that they should handle this sugar packet any differently than normal. What you'll see now is that when someone grabs for one of these tube-shaped packets, they shake it, break it, and pour it, just like they did with the square packages. They use the new technology with old knowledge. The people getting coffee from Starbucks didn't have a problem putting sugar in their coffee, so there was no need for a solution.

On the other hand, sugar packets have been a standard size for quite some time, particularly in my home country of Italy. What I began to increasingly observe there was that as people became more aware of their sugar intake, they would only pour about half the packet of sugar into their coffee and throw the other half away—either that, or the half-used bag remained on the table, likely spilling and causing further inconvenience. What I see today are smaller packets—a much better solution to an actual problem for people who want to use less sugar. And if you have a sweet tooth, you can simply use two packets.

The tube packet is arguably a superior solution to the square packet; that does not make it a *better* solution. What consumers look for in a sugar packet tends to be the same for everyone. In some cases, however, there are different types of users with different needs.

YOUR VERY OWN WAY TO FLY

Most airlines approach business from an operations standpoint, meaning that they want the flights to be efficient and the service to be pleasant, but that experience is entirely driven by the company. Avianca Airlines, instead, is attempting to understand who their passengers are as well as their wants and needs—so they began to research.

They found that the most relevant information about the passengers was whether or not they could book their trips on their own or if they needed assistance. Depending on which category they fell into, Avianca designed a different experience journey for them. If the passenger needs assistance, they receive support. If they buy the ticket independently, then the process is much smoother for them.

The second dimension they analyzed was whether or not the passengers wanted a standardized service. They started considering: What are the things the passenger truly cares about and values? Is it being on time or having a comfortable seat? Do they need rest or do they need flexibility of schedule? With the answers to these questions, Avianca is designing entirely different traveling experiences that match the expectations and needs of each of their passengers.

When you catch a plane, you know that the passenger sitting next to you has almost certainly paid a different price than you for what appears like the same service: flying from A to B. You paid a different price, because "going from A to B" really means different things for you and the other passenger. Avianca will ensure you also have an overall unique flight experience, and one that meets your individual expectations.

Once again, the value of this approach is that it accelerates learning in the face of complex problems with uncertain solutions. Responsive Decision Making does not only apply to startup (lean) or new products and solutions (design thinking). It can be cultivated throughout the life of a company.

For example, Facebook was not launched to be a global platform. It started as a small-scale experiment at Harvard University. As it developed, they added new features, and the platform expanded. They learned as rapidly as possible, and the totality of the Facebook experience was progressively implemented through cycles, a process called agile management.

AGILE MANAGEMENT

When personal computers emerged in the 1980s, they helped create a new management style called "empowerment management," where users and employees felt empowered to make autonomous decisions. In the 1990s, the emergence of collaborative software triggered the knowledge management movement.

The most recent iteration of this trend is agile management, a managerial approach that involves constant innovation and a constant process of improvement. It asks us not to make long-term plans but to undergo numerous cycles of improvements.

Agile management is built on a few critical principles—that it's necessary to engage with users to better understand them; that rapid prototyping techniques are important; and that the need to test these prototypes on the market by collaborating with users to understand their value is strong. It's a matter of mind and attitude rather than a set of procedures. Agile management emphasizes improvising to develop prototyping until a viable business model emerges, and this methodology has become more common.

This type of agile management is quite effective in situations where customer preferences and abilities change frequently. It's also an important tool with more unpredictable markets, such as internet-based services or tech companies—but even in more stable markets such as higher education and oil and gas, agile management can still prove useful.

AGILE MANIFESTO

After the frustrations of developing software with the traditional approach, seventeen thought leaders issued the Agile Manifesto[15] in 2001. The Manifesto reads:

We are uncovering better ways of developing software by doing it and helping others do it. Through this work we have come to value:

- Individuals and interactions over processes and tools
- Working software over comprehensive documentation
- Customer collaboration over contract negotiation
- Responding to change over following a plan

That is, while there is value in the items on the right, we value the items on the left more.

---

15 https://agilemanifesto.org/

KEEP LEARNING

Embrace a learning-driven attitude and it will penetrate your entire organization. Don't avoid those mistakes, because you are avoiding an opportunity to learn. Keep going to work as if it were day one.

What happens on day two?

In the words of Jeff Bezos,[16] "Day two is stasis. Followed by irrelevance. Followed by excruciating, painful decline. Followed by death."

When you try to do something new, you're bound to fail because, by definition, you don't know yet how to do new things. However, there are not many companies where making mistakes to learn is part of their code, or even considered acceptable—and so most people try to avoid making mistakes and hide them if they make any.

At a company I was working with, the internet site crashed in the middle of their largest promotional sale ever. Millions were lost in missed sales. Obviously, everyone involved was frustrated. In most companies, when something like this happens, the natural reaction is for everyone to duck and cover to avoid being caught in the rage from management. Management looks for someone to scapegoat and determines whether or not they need to be working there anymore. Everybody looks for a place to hide.

---

16 "Amazon Shareholders Teaches Some Extraordinary Lessons in Leadership," Inc., last modified April 20, 2017, https://www.inc.com/justin-bariso/20-years-ago-amazons-jeff-bezos-sent-an-extraordinary-letter-to-shareholders.html.

Instead, this company had the opposite attitude. They accepted this mistake as a unique opportunity to learn how to do things better. Instead of looking for someone to punish, they dissected the situation to determine exactly what had happened so they could avoid such an instance in the future. They turned the site crash into the single most useful event of the week—perhaps even the year.

GET OUT OF YOUR OWN WAY

If you've read until this point, I am confident you will have appreciated how useful CLEVER is to you and your company. I can now make a confession. I did not invent CLEVER.

You did.

Or at least many professionals like you. I did not sit up in my office late at night imagining what my readers would need. I've asked them. I've discussed these concepts with hundreds of executives, managers, entrepreneurs, colleagues, and students, refining the framework and polishing it over six years, to clearly gauge what *they* thought I should write in this book.

The biggest obstacle for me was not embracing a Responsive Decision Making approach. It was accepting the reason why it is necessary. The reason is that I am not as clever as I would like to be. Most people aren't.

When you have a hypothesis about your business, of course you want it to be true. You think, "I'm so clever. I had this brilliant intuition. It has to be correct." What happens then is that you fall so deeply in love with your own idea that you're not willing to learn that your idea might not have been so good to begin with.

The truth is that there is nothing wrong with your first idea not being good enough, so long as you can improve on it fast enough that it *becomes* great. That must be your attitude in the face of VUCA.

QUESTIONS

1. What would you do differently if your company did not exist and you wanted to create it from scratch today?
2. How do your products and services help your customers succeed at what they care about?
3. What experiments could you run to cheaply and quickly explore new ways to meet your customers' needs?
4. In your company, who makes the decision to launch a new product and the features it should have?
5. Does your company run a few long, high-stakes projects or many short, iterative ones?
6. What was the mistake you've made or witnessed somebody else making this year from which you've learned the most?

CHAPTER 8

CLEVER STRATEGY

O ur theme for this entire journey together is that the world is changing faster than ever. Consequently, the rules of strategy have changed. The purpose of CLEVER is to guide you through the new drivers for strategic success. Yet, making different decisions also requires making decisions differently. This chapter in particular is designed to help you think about those strategic decisions in a new way fit for the 4IR.

We'll explore this in parts—for established companies and for startups—in order to bring together all of this information in a useful way. For established companies, we will address the executives as well as middle managers. We will also take a look at established family businesses. For each of these positions, the questions become: how do you embrace this framework, set your strategic plans, and implement them?

CLEVER FOR EXECUTIVES

As a senior executive or a c-suite officer, it is your responsibility to ensure a strategy that will keep the company successful in the future. How do you do that?

If you manage a successful company, don't stop what you're doing right now. Over the next few years, most of your company's revenues will come from the exact same sources as last year. You should develop your products and services and make them better. For example, every two or three years, automobile manufacturers have a slight redesign of each model; then they add a few additional options; and then they release a limited-edition color; and so on.

But this won't be enough forever.

So, at the same time, you need to think about how they're going to make money twenty or thirty years from now and they have to start preparing because, at the current pace of technological progress, over the next twenty-five years we will experience a century's worth of innovation.[1] Nobody's waiting.

---

1   Ray Kurzweil, "The Law of Accelerating Returns," Kurzweil, last modified March 7, 2001, https://www.kurzweilai.net/the-law-of-accelerating-returns.

The products, services, and business models that performed well until today will inevitably decline and be replaced by new products, services, and business models fit for a new era. Figure 7[2] represents the interlocking paths of the decline of old models and emergence of new ones. The 1st Horizon describes current offerings and models that have been successful but are not really future proof. This is the carmakers' biyearly redesign and incremental upgrade. Yet, in an age of autonomous vehicles, selling a limited-edition sedan will not keep a company successful. You can't ignore the 1st Horizon, as this is what keeps your company going, but you shouldn't focus on this only.

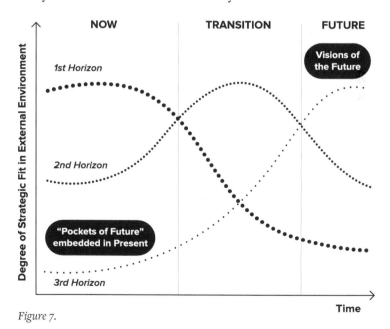

Figure 7.

---

2   Andrew Curry, Tony Hodgson, "Seeing in Multiple Horizons: Connecting Futures to Strategy," *Journal of Futures Studies*, August 2008, 13(1): 1-20

For example, advisory company IDC estimates that 60 percent of the world GDP will be digitized by 2022.[3] What that suggests is that non-digitized GDP, based on the technologies from the last industrial revolution, will quickly shrink to 40 percent globally, and less than that in advanced economies. Their decline will continue until their contribution to global GDP is undetectable. They will morph into anecdotes from corporate prehistory passed down by older employees:

"When I was your age, we did that *by hand*!"

Knowing that some things will no longer work is interesting. Yet, it'd be more useful to know what the future holds and what will work in its stead.

What will work on the 2nd Horizon, that is five, seven, or ten years from now?

Most people can't really answer. Will autonomous vehicles circulate in most cities in five, seven, or ten years? Not sure. Will renewable energy be affordable without subsidies in five, seven, or ten years? Not sure. Will robots or 3-D printing transform manufacturing in five, seven, or ten years? Not sure.

Such uncertainty can be paralyzing. Yet, this is the time horizon for most critical strategic decisions. There are two ways to solve this paralysis. The first is to look backwards from an even more distant future.

---

3 "IDC FutureScape: Multiplied Innovation Takes Off, Powered by AI, Distributed Public Cloud, Microservices, Developer Population Explosion, Greater Specialization and Verticalization, and Scaling Trust," IDC, last modified October 30, 2018, https://www.idc.com/getdoc.jsp?containerId=prUS44417618.

Quite interestingly, most of these near-future uncertainties seem to dissipate when we look at the 3rd Horizon, that is twenty or thirty years ahead. Almost everyone is confident that all the vehicles will be autonomous; that robots will have taken over 4D jobs (dull, dirty, dangerous, and dear, from chapter 2); that abundant energy from renewable sources will be widely available; that personalized healthcare and education will be affordable; that advanced AI, 3-D printing, and immersive computing will be ubiquitous...

Are they correct?

Nobody knows. We cannot predict the future,[4] because it does not exist yet. In fact, we normally talk about *the futures*,[5] to acknowledge that many different trajectories are possible.

Interestingly, though most of these futures will never exist, we can learn something useful from them. If you are confident about the long-term future, then the strategic decisions you must make in the 2nd Horizon are those that will position your company to win during the 3rd Horizon. This entails preparing your company for a turbulent, fast changing world of ubiquitous technology. CLEVER will assist you in doing so. The CLEVER framework contains the strategic drivers that prepare your company to master the digital futures.

---

4   Jim Dator, "What Futures Studies Is, and Is Not," accessed October 21, 2019, http://www.futures.hawaii.edu/publications/futures-studies/WhatFSis1995.pdf

5   Jennifer Gidley, *The Future: A Very Short Introduction* (New York: Oxford University Press, 2017).

The second way to overcome the paralyzing uncertainty of the 2nd Horizon is to look from the present into the future and gauge where it is headed. Indeed, most of the new products, services, and business models that will succeed in the near future are already all around us. Some are still gaining acceptance; others are still being fine-tuned; they all are on a fast path to the new mainstream. As the cyberpunk author William Gibson famously said, "The future is already here—it's just not very evenly distributed."

As an executive, you should identify the emerging products, services, and business models that are increasingly fit for the new era. Once again, CLEVER will assist you in doing so. The CLEVER framework maps and analyses the emerging strategic drivers that help you master the 4IR.

THE PURSUIT OF INNOVATION

Executives should manage a pipeline of innovations—a portfolio of sorts. They should simultaneously target three time horizons—the near term future to remain profitable, the midterm future to keep growing, and the long-term future to ensure relevance and survival. I'm not suggesting you should allocate your resources equally across the time horizons. The most successful companies[6] invest about 70 percent on core projects that deliver results in the 1st Horizon and about 20 percent on projects for the 2nd Horizon. Only about 10 percent of budgets are

---

6   Bansi Nagji and Geoff Tuff, "Managing Your Innovation Portfolio," *Harvard Business Review* (May 2012), accessed October 21, 2019, https://hbr.org/2012/05/managing-your-innovation-portfolio.

destined for strategic initiatives for the 3rd Horizon. Yet, over time, these initiatives are responsible for 70 percent of the returns.

Yet, this is not only a decision about budget allocation.

When I work with senior management in companies, I'm often asked, "What should we do to be more innovative to get ready for the Fourth Industrial Revolution?" The truth is that most of the time, that is the wrong question. The right question would be, "What should we *stop doing* that prevents us from being innovative?" The most common answers[7] are: punishing useful mistakes, rewarding compliance with rules instead of problem-solving, allocating insufficient resources, focusing on short-term results, considering innovation a task for R&D only, micromanaging employees, and keeping them in the dark regarding strategy.

This is hard for most leaders, especially during difficult times, because when they see a problem, particularly a slowdown in growth, they focus on profit margins. They enter into a panic mode and immediately start cutting costs and tightening their grip on employees, instead of making investments and creating the conditions to grow again.

If you recognize this problem, then you should look for two things: ways to organize innovation inside the organization and how to leverage innovations that are happening outside the organization.

---

7   H. Soken, Nelson, and B. Kim Barnes, "What Kills Innovation? Your Role as a Leader in Supporting an Innovative Culture," *Industrial and Commercial Training* 46, no. 1 (January 28, 2014): 7–15, https://doi.org/10.1108/ict-09-2013-0057.

There are many methods and models to innovate internally and externally, but the general agreement is that internal innovation tends to be incremental. It improves on existing features of products; it does not redefine industries. External innovation works better for radical or disruptive innovation, and these are the innovations that change the rules of the game.

All the organizations I work with have research and development departments, lead cross-functional and team innovation projects, run internal incubation programs, or manage a combination of the above. You might also see innovation days where people are challenged to find solutions to problems or improve company offerings. These are all excellent ways for companies to pursue internal innovation. Fewer companies, however, pursue external innovation with equal determination.

I like to approach this issue with two truly eye-opening questions by Allison Davis and Matthew Le Merle.[8] The first is: over the next decade, where are the most important innovations in our industry coming from? Most of us would love to answer that those innovations will come from within our company. In my experience, however, a great majority of respondents admit that the most interesting and valuable innovations will originate not only outside their company, but even outside their industry.

The follow-up question, then, is: how much of the

---

8 Matthew C. Le Merle and Alison Davis, *Corporate Innovation in the Fifth Era: Lessons from Alphabet/Google, Amazon, Apple, Facebook and Microsoft* (Corte Madera, CA: Cartwright Publishing, 2017).

innovation budget is spent internally versus externally? In my experiences, most companies spend 70 percent or more internally, despite the fact that most of the innovation is coming from the outside. Too many companies are passively waiting for potential threats to play out before responding and systematically miss out on the opportunities to invest in extraordinary innovations.

One path to innovation that comes from an external source is engaging with outside experts. This can be an advisory board made of people outside your industry, or you can participate in a collective initiative at the industry level. Many CEOs give talks and participate in industry level initiatives or societal level initiatives as it is a means of exchanging ideas at the forefront of innovation. The World Economic Forum offers a unique forum to engage in this type of exchange. At one workshop in Mexico City, I facilitated a co-creation session, where the chairman of one of Mexico's largest corporations, a former minister in the Mexican Government, and the executive director of a global NGO came up with the idea for a new initiative to fight corruption. The initiative was later successfully launched and received international recognition and awards for its originality and impact.

There are also incubation and acceleration programs that you can actively collaborate with, to stay abreast of what's new in the startup world. I've accompanied many corporate delegations to such venues. Such opportunities provide you with access to what might be the next disruptive technology and afford you the chance to collaborate with new clients, suppliers, and partners. The single greatest takeaway for corporate visitors is invariably the honesty with which start-ups discuss failure and accept mistakes.

Sometimes companies engage in collaboration because there's always a risk that radically new innovations won't work. They share the risk associated with the project's failure. For example, all autonomous vehicles are being developed by consortia of companies that collaborate to innovate together. A related reason is that the stakes are increasingly high. High-profile incidents like an autonomous vehicle car crash, for example, can be damaging to the value and reputation of a company. By partnering with small startups, companies risk less damage to their own name because they can develop under an alternate brand. If the product is ready to be released into the world, they acknowledge or acquire the startup, and the project is placed under the umbrella of the head corporation.

As an executive, your role is critical in embracing the CLEVER framework. You can use the six strategic drivers to pursue innovative initiatives, coming from different sources and aimed at different time horizons. Yet more, you are in a position to promote a CLEVER culture in your organization. This is bound to be your greatest legacy.

CLEVER FOR FAMILY BUSINESSES

The problems family businesses encounter are numerous and unique. Family businesses are torn by the need to find a balance between two dimensions—the business and the family, which are intrinsically different. Family is driven by cooperation and a socialistic spirit, whereas a business is driven by competition and a capitalistic spirit. With family, you want to keep everything close and private—you want to control it. In business, you have to open up and share information with others. Family tends to be risk averse and make decisions based on emotions and effect, whereas in business, you must take risks and make decisions based on rationality. Families also tend to be a bit more conservative with their money—they want to save. Businesses are driven by investment. Families are more focused on tradition—businesses need to change.

You get the idea.

The question is—which one is better? For family businesses, the answer is: both are equally important. Interestingly enough, most family businesses find creative and original ways to strike a balance. These dimensions seem to be in contradiction with each other, but in fact they are not strictly in conflict—they are, according to John Ward[9], Amy Schuman, and Stacy Stutz, a paradox. Family businesses find ways to cooperate while they compete—to be rational while they're driven by their emotions.

This makes family businesses well-positioned and well-suited to succeed in the current ambiguous business environment. However, not every tension is simply a paradox that can be reconciled in a creative manner. Sooner or later,

---

9   Amy Schuman, Stacy Stutz, and John L. Ward, *Family Business as Paradox* (Hampshire, England: Palgrave Macmillan, 2010).

family businesses require that you make a choice between three systems—the business dimension, the family dimension, and the ownership dimension or structure.

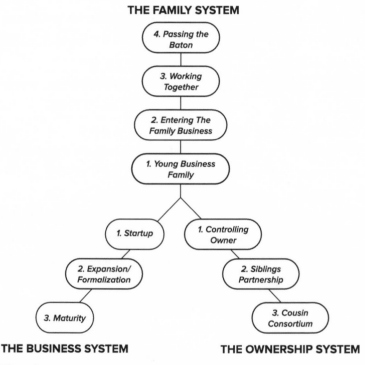

Figure 8.

Figure 8[10] shows how these dimensions progress over time. The business begins as a startup where everything is probably a bit confused. There are no structures or policies, and everything is done by the family—the founder and

---

10 K. Gersick, J. Davis, M. Hampton & I. Lansberg (1997). *Generation to Generation: Life Cycle of the Family Business*. Harvard Business School Press)

their spouse, the siblings, or whoever is doing whatever needs to be done.

As the business grows, there is a need to make it more formalized and professional. There must be rules in place, along with different people to carry out different responsibilities. When the business is mature, it is managed professionally, and the founders no longer make all of the decisions.

The family system usually starts out with a small, young business family. As it grows, some additional family members join the business until it becomes a family business proper. They work together for some time until the founders need to move on and let the next generations take the helm.

The ownership system continues in a similar vein. In the beginning, the owner owns and controls every aspect of the business. Then there are siblings that work together, and then their children. The grandchildren of the founder eventually manage what is called the "cousin consortium."

If everything goes well and the three dimensions progress more or less at the same pace, it is easier to balance the evolution of the family business, but there are times when the things you want to achieve for the sake of the family are in contradiction with the things you want to do for the sake of the business. For example, do you want to keep every family member in the business and give them all managerial positions because that's what's good for the family, or do you want to hire professional managers because that's what's good for the business? Do you want everyone to have the same shares that allow them to have decision-making power because that's what's best for the family, or should those who have the greatest capabilities of running the business have them? Should you focus on building family assets by saving money or should you pursue the growth of the business?

It is my contention that while these things become a bit tricky, when you have to make a decision between the interest of the family or the interest of the business, your role requires that you always do what's best for the business, no matter how uncomfortable or painful is the decision. Without the business, there is no family business—whereas the family, in a sense, will always be there. Putting the business first means not defending what you've always done just because it was the way your grandfather did it. It means keeping what you have while investing in the near-term with an eye on the more distant time horizon.

When my students who come from family businesses— particularly ones that have been successful for decades— go home from taking my courses where they learn about CLEVER, they suggest to their parents or grandparents new ways to embrace the framework. More often than not, the response is along the lines of, "We've been doing this successfully for a century. Why do we have to change now?" It's a fair question, but it's perhaps not the most relevant. What I find to be a more important question is, "If we could start from scratch today, would we do the same things we started doing one hundred years ago?" If they're honest with themselves, they'd probably say no, because whatever they did that was smart and successful one hundred years ago is very unlikely to be fit for the VUCA world of 4IR.

During a workshop I held for a pharmaceutical multinational, whose regional distributors are by and large family businesses, we discussed the obstacles to investing in more innovation. A common answer was that the next generation was not interested in working with the family business. Why? They had more exciting career options in fast-growing corporations, global banks and consulting firms, and innovative startups around the world. That is a pity.

As the head of a family business, you must ensure the long-term success of your family company. It is a huge responsibility, both towards the past and the future generations. The CLEVER framework is designed to help you think precisely on that timeframe. You should not make decisions bound only by the past trajectory of your business. Create a business that your children and their children will be proud of and excited to work in.

CLEVER FOR ENTREPRENEURS

Many of the entrepreneurs I work with come to see me on our very first meeting with the idea that their startup must have a fully developed product, with complex advanced features. They also usually have already hired a designer to create a cool logo and are working on their internet site. I admire their determination, but all of these things are secondary. A startup is not a tiny version of a company. So, it doesn't need all these company-like widgets. A startup is much more similar to a laboratory—a set of experiments that you run to test whether or not you have the ability to put together a product for which there is a market and that makes such market happy.

Companies tend to be structured and conservative environments. They are run professionally with hierarchies, policies, and procedures in place—all distractions from the more important things you need to do as a fledgling business:

Identify the right customer and serve them to start growing.

In the process, you might modify your initial idea, say, from matching companies and job applicants in the UK to offering executive education in India. Impossible? This is based on the true story of a startup—launched by two brilliant entrepreneurs and later personal friends—I've collaborated with and invested in. Andrea Bonaceto, the former CEO, has since moved on to launch one of the world's first blockchain investment funds.[11] Krishna Venkata is now spearheading the next pivot, providing outsourced advanced software development in Bangalore.

There is no shame in pivoting or changing trajectory. This is the essence of learning and embracing Responsive Decision Making. In fact, it'd be shameful to stubbornly stick to a failing business model, without changing it. Even the great success stories of entrepreneurship have gone through some pivots.

---

11 Celia Pearce, "Alumni Case Study: The Future of Blockchain Technology," Imperial College Business School, last modified May 22, 2018, https://www.imperial.ac.uk/business-school/intelligence/alumni/alumni-case-study-the-future-of-blockchain-technology/.

For example, PayPal began by offering payments for the people who used a PalmPilot, a handheld computer that was the precursor to the smartphone. They created a payment system that lets users beam payments to others. Soon they realized there were too few PalmPilots around and that users had no interest in the service. At the same time, they had established an internet site to support the service, and they recognized that people were instead quite happy to use that site to make payments for other users.

Though the initial idea of PayPal as a PalmPilot payment system failed, they realized that there was a demand for it to become an email-based payment system. So, they changed it. Responsive Decision Making at its best. Once they did that, they tapped into a new market and exploded. When you're small and find that new market, a few things can happen.

One is that you find you don't have the ability to stay in business because you don't make enough money initially. Another is that competitors make their way in and you lose the bigger opportunities to them. In response, many startups try to grow slowly and responsibly. This would have been the wise strategy in a more stable, slower, and predictable world. In today's VUCA times, Reid Hoffman[12] has a different suggestion. As the CEO and founder of LinkedIn and part of the initial team at PayPal, Hoffman is a leading authority on fast-growing startups.

---

12 Reid Hoffman and Chris Yeh, *Blitzscaling: The Lightning-Fast Path to Building Massively Valuable Companies* (New York: Currency, 2018).

His advice is that at that stage, instead of fixing all the problems that come, instead of trying to have as much strategy as you can and grow moderately, you should grow at hyper speed—a type of growth he calls "blitzscaling." If you do, you conquer the market, and then that market is yours forever. For both PayPal and LinkedIn this proved especially important, because they operated a platform and, as we discussed in chapter 5, the most important asset for a platform is a large network of users. If you lock the users in, then you have a strong competitive position. Later you can take the time to fix the problems because you will be making enough money to fix whatever needs fixing.

What's interesting about this idea is that if you do attempt to fix a problem as a small startup and then define a policy for that problem, your solution will likely be obsolete when your startup grows. So, it would have been a waste of time or, worse, turn into a burden.

Imagine you have a dinner party where you invite three to four of your friends. You call them to confirm, you make your grocery lists, you buy the products, stock the refrigerator, commence to cooking, and your friends arrive. Now imagine the same scenario, but with fifteen people attending. The things that made sense for you to do in the previous scale with three to four friends no longer make sense. You don't call each one of them to confirm. You likely book a restaurant instead of choosing to cook yourself, and you make sure it's a restaurant that most of them will like.

Now imagine you have to do this for one hundred people. Now a restaurant won't suffice—you'll have to book a venue and hire a catering service. The catering only handles the food, so when it comes to confirming the guest list, you won't be able to confirm who attended until afterwards due to the sheer number.

Now imagine 5,000 people. Now imagine 100,000.

This is what happens when startups grow. The types of problems they must address and the nature of managing the business morph into something else entirely. Finding solutions to early problems is in all likelihood a waste of time, because those same problems probably won't exist as you continue to grow.

I deeply love the energy of entrepreneurs. I love mentoring them and working with them. It's a journey that started a decade ago, when I founded and managed a business incubator in Italy. That entrepreneurial experience has taught me many things about entrepreneurship, some self-evident, some very profound. One lesson I hold dear is that entrepreneurship is ultimately a human experience. It's an exercise in grit and even unreasonableness to repeatedly overcome insurmountable problems. It cannot be achieved alone. It requires partners, friends, employees, mentors, and investors. These supportive stakeholders also have expectations that can create incredible pressure.

While we always seem eager to celebrate entrepreneurship and startups, we do not talk enough about this pressure. When I was invited to the G20's Youth Engagement Initiative in Argentina, I realized that the seventy-odd young talents in my audience were constantly exposed to words of excitement and encouragement towards entrepreneurship. So, I decided to warn against the pitfalls. In my talk, I reminded them that 90 percent[13] of the startups fail, including 75 percent[14] of the most promising and best-funded, which have attracted venture capital investments. I also prepared them that entrepreneurs must cope with such pressure that half of them experience mental health problems.[15] Yet, the rewards of successful entrepreneurship, when human ingenuity and greatness create value, are a true joy to behold.

As an entrepreneur you have a responsibility to create value for your customers, your team, and your investors. At first you won't be sure if what you plan to do works, you will run a lab of sorts in order to find out. As soon as that is clear, you may need to grow incredibly fast. When doing so, you will have to accept making poor decisions, being inefficient and wasting resources, just so that you can grow, because after you've grown, many of the problems will have become irrelevant. In fact, your company will grow so fast that it will be radically transformed every few months.

For example, Careem, the startup we discussed in chapters 5 and 6, was growing at 30 percent a month. This means that it doubled in size every two and a half months. Every

13 Max Marmer, Bjoern Lasse Hermann, Ertan Dogrultan, and Ron Berman, "Startup Genome Report Extra on Premature Scaling," last modified August 29, 2011, http://innovationfootprints.com/wp-content/uploads/2015/07/startup-genome-report-extra-on-premature-scaling.pdf.

14 Deborah Gage, "The Venture Capital Secret: 3 Out of 4 Start-Ups Fail," *The Wall Street Journal*, last modified September 20, 2012, https://www.wsj.com/articles/SB10000872396390443720204578004980476429190.

15 Michael A. Freeman, Sheri Johnson, and Paige Staudenmaier, "Are Entrepreneurs 'Touched with Fire'?" last modified April 17, 2015, www.michaelafreemanmd.com/Research.html.

six months, new employees were more than all the previous employees. If you do the math, you will conclude that Careem was growing twenty-three times per year. Whatever solution seems fit for your startup now, it will be inadequate when you're twenty-three times larger just twelve months from now.

Throughout this overwhelming pressure to firefight, cope with change, and continue to grow, you must keep the strategic course straight. CLEVER will keep your eyes on the deep strategic drivers that affect your long-term success.

CLEVER FOR INTRAPRENEURS: MIDDLE MANAGERS AND JUNIOR FAMILY MEMBERS

Middle managers are in a unique position where they have frequent interaction with suppliers, customers, colleagues, and peers. Their interaction with these various stakeholders gives them distinctive insight and knowledge that a CEO simply wouldn't have. They are the most likely candidates for bringing CLEVER ideas to senior management.

A very famous example is the middle managers at FedEx, the express shipping company, who developed a plan to create many more drop off points for packages by installing drop boxes on all FedEx vans. That way, if a customer sees a FedEx van, they can simply drop off their parcel on the spot. This idea didn't come from Joe Parron, the CEO. Rather, it was birthed in the middle. Another legendary example comes from 3M, the company that invented Post-it Notes. Post-It Notes are the silver-lining of a failed innovation.

Engineers at the company were trying to develop a new glue, but the substance turned out to not be very effective. Instead of abandoning the project, one of the engineers tried to turn the weakness of the glue into a strength. He pitched the idea of an adhesive that allows people to easily stick and unstick small sheets of paper. This product, the Post-It, became a resounding success and a signature product for the company.

This type of innovation from 3M should not come as a surprise. The company is famous for allowing employees to spend up to 20 percent of their working hours pursuing new projects of their own choice. Google does something similar. That's how Gmail was invented. Companies that recognize the importance of strategic ideas coming from lower and middle management end up innovating in ways that have terrific impact on the markets they serve.

However, it's often difficult for middle-managers and junior family members to raise issues of strategy with their superiors. Many companies and families don't have a culture of innovation that fosters these exchanges, are risk-averse, or simply assume that expecting strategic decisions must originate at the top levels of the organization. It's impossible for middle managers to single-handedly change the culture of an organization—instead, they should work around it. They need to become "intrapreneurs."[16] Intrapreneurs are like entrepreneurs in that they are innovators and

16 Jordan Daykin, "Intrapreneurship." *Forbes*, last modified January 8, 2019, https://www.forbes.com/sites/jordandaykin/2019/01/08/intrapreneurship/#56465aa94ea3.

change-makers, but they do so within an existing organization instead of forming their own companies.

MAKING THE CASE FOR CLEVER

Let's say that you work in a more traditional company that does not have a culture of innovation. You must find other ways to promote change. That doesn't mean cornering your boss in the lunchroom and demanding they do x, y, or z, or lecturing him on how smart you really are. Rather, there are techniques and strategies that have been proven to work in persuading upper management to pursue change and innovation.

The idea of pitching[17] an idea to upper management is called "issue selling."[18] You're persuading them to do something that they may be reluctant to even consider. When approaching this kind of situation, it's important to think about it in the same way one does Responsive Decision Making. One of the most important concepts covered in the last chapter was the necessity of understanding the perspective of the user. If you're in middle management, in this scenario, the "user" you're persuading to adopt new ideas is senior management. If it's a family business, perhaps you're pitching it to your parents or grandparents. Whoever the audience is, before

---

17 Susan J. Ashford and James R. Detert, "Get the Boss to Buy In." *Harvard Business Review* (January-February 2015), accessed October 21, 2019, https://hbr.org/2015/01/get-the-boss-to-buy-in.

18 Lauren Keller Johnson, "Issue Selling in the Organization." *MIT Sloan Management Review* (Spring 2012), last modified April 15, 2002, https://sloanreview.mit.edu/article/strategy-issue-selling-in-the-organization/.

pitching a solution to anyone, you need to understand what their position is, what their expectations are, what type of person they are, and how they see different challenges.

Is your company worried about the competition or are they focused on ways of growing revenue and profitability? You need to link one, or all six, drivers of CLEVER to ongoing strategic issues that your company is prioritizing. You should be providing a solution to a problem your boss or your parents already perceive as urgent. It is too soon for you to put items on the strategy agenda, but it's not too soon to help address the items that senior management has already put there.

Another important element for the acceptance of an idea is your understanding of your organization. In different organizations, you should approach people differently. For example, in some places an informal conversation followed up by an email may be preferred, when others might require an appointment for a formal pitch. In many cases, it's best to approach a decision maker privately as opposed to pitching something in a meeting or public forum with an audience, where they might be under pressure. There's no template for a solution that works in all places. You must analyze and act on these factors in a way that you view as making the best impression.

According to research, there are two major strategies for successful issue selling: bundling an idea together with other strategic issues, as mentioned above, and choosing the right people and channels, either public or private, to propose your idea.

In this respect, a team effort to push an idea can be more productive than a single person doing so, and there are a few different people you could involve in your plan. One option is to reach out to someone above you, like your boss or their superior. If the superior of your boss understands the value of what you are proposing, they might make it a priority for your direct boss. This is one way to get your proposal to the next level, although you will have to consider office politics carefully. Peers and people at a lower level can also be helpful allies. If an idea comes from multiple sides, it's often perceived as being more important and relevant.

Senior management also responds favorably to "expert" opinions. It's more likely your boss will give you the green light if you bring in an external expert, like a consultant or a professor that your boss finds credible and who recommends the same course of action[19] as you wanted to "sell."

A PERFECT PITCH TO PERSUADE YOUR BOSS

A perfect pitch is structured into five parts—gap, purpose, capabilities, organizational support, and benefits. Research[20] has shown that the inclusion of these five elements boosts the likelihood that your message will be well received and that your solution will be implemented.

19 Susan J. Ashford and James R. Detert, "Get the Boss to Buy In." *Harvard Business Review* (January-February 2015), accessed October 21, 2019, https://hbr.org/2015/01/get-the-boss-to-buy-in.

20 Matthew J. Mazzei, Christopher L. Shook, David J. Ketchen, "Selling Strategic Issues: Crafting the Content of the Sales Pitch" *Business Horizons*, 52 (6): 539-543

The pitch should begin by highlighting the gap between the ideal and the current situation, showing your audience there is a problem.

Second, you show that the idea you are pitching can bridge that gap and fix the issue. This is the purpose.

Third, after revealing the problem and proposing a solution, you must persuade your audience that your team has the capability to successfully implement the proposed idea.

Fourth, you demonstrate that you have the right organizational support. This might mean showing that you can count on your boss's superior, or the other colleagues and peers who are on board.

Finally, it's essential to display the value and benefits that come along with the successful implementation of your solution.

You can further improve[21] your pitch by making sure that your idea is really new, by including a prototype, demo, or physical object which clearly conveys the solution you are suggesting, and by using influencing tactics, like asking the boss what she thinks or offering to help with the implementation.

As an intrapreneur in a company or in your family business, you must help your organization stay relevant and successful over time. This is not only what you want because it will get you promoted. It should be what you wish for because you want to work for a successful organization.

---

21 "How to Score Big When Pitching an Idea to the Boss," AOM Insights, accessed October 21, 2019, https://journals.aom.org/doi/10.5465/amj.2016.0942.summary.

This is your foremost responsibility. It's the reason you were hired in the first place. You must share with the executive team the unique insights you gain from your perspective and help them take a more comprehensive view of the changing competitive landscape. CLEVER helps you frame your ideas and position them not as mere intuitions, but as strategic plans for the continued success of your company.

GO FORWARD WITH CONFIDENCE

As mentioned in the introduction of this book, you may choose to employ one, a few, or all of CLEVER's strategic drivers. How do you know what is right for your company?

When it comes to pursuing the six strategic drivers of CLEVER inside an organization, we must distinguish between the first three letters and the last three. The CLE of CLEVER—Collaborative Intelligence, Learning Systems, and Exponential Technologies—are all ongoing technological trends currently happening outside organizations and ecosystems. The VER—Value Facilitation, Ethical Championship, and Responsible Decision Making—are about the managerial decisions and the culture within an organization. Strategies that leverage all of CLEVER are not automatically the best ones. A strategy only works when it helps leaders bring their company where they want it to be in the future.

How do you craft a strategy for a digital future?

One of the things that most companies do not understand about digital strategies and the digital transformation that ensues is that it is not about the technology—those change faster than you can imagine, and when they change, they quickly become obsolete. If your company adapts its strategy to a specific technology, that too will soon be obsolete.

Digital transformation is an opportunity to do things differently and become better at managing change. Digital transformation is a cultural transformation in disguise. It is about changes in mindset, not adapting to technological trends. Once you realize that, you'll find your ability to accept and navigate change greatly improved. Then, CLEVER will assist you in making the right strategic decisions.

You are now armed with the tools you need to confidently help your company navigate these VUCA times. It won't be easy—revolutions never are—but with the right research and support, I am confident you will master the 4IR.

QUESTION

1. In the face of the accelerating change, how do you want your company to be different in the next five years?

CONCLUSION

Let's close this book by discussing a company that everybody knows and that clearly illustrates every aspect of CLEVER—Uber.

Started in 2009, Uber went public in 2019, with a valuation of $82 billion[1] and an expected, longer-term valuation of $100 billion.[2] Uber radically transformed the taxi and chauffeur industry, without being a car or a transportation company. So, the incumbents did not see it coming. It launched as a mobile app for ride hailing, but its operations and

1   Rob Davies, "Uber Valued at $82.4bn as It Prices IPO at $45 per Share," *The Guardian*, last modified May 9, 2019, https://www.theguardian.com/business/2019/may/09/uber-value-wall-street-ipo-friday.
2   "Uber is on the Right Path to $100 Billion Valuation, Analyst Ives Says," *Bloomberg*, last modified June 6, 2019, https://www.bloomberg.com/news/videos/2019-06-06/uber-is-on-the-right-path-to-100-billion-valuation-analyst-ives-says-video.

strategy are not defined by an industry—they are defined by what it can do. Uber's technology allowed them to expand into many other areas.

Uber now also delivers food, rents bikes and scooters, ships freight, transports patients to hospitals, and in some cities, offers aerial transportation. These are seemingly different industries, but the competencies for success are the same. And this is, arguably, just the beginning.

CLEVER IN ACTION

Uber embodies the spirit of CLEVER in many ways. It's an excellent example of how to employ the framework, but it's also a good lens to think about where companies can go wrong.

C: COLLABORATIVE INTELLIGENCE

Uber employs the different skills of humans and Learning Systems in tandem. When you hail a ride with the app, the system contacts the nearest driver to you and links you to them in real time. This could never be achieved by human intelligence alone. Even accurately identifying the driver nearest to the rider would be a major hurdle. Yet you still need humans to drive the cars, help with luggage, interface with clients, and to do other tasks that robots can't achieve—yet.

L: LEARNING SYSTEMS

Uber uses Learning Systems for numerous tasks. They collect data about riders and the journeys they take to make predictions about future supply and demand. They ride a fine balance between making sure there is never too long a wait time for a ride and that there aren't too many drivers on the road. If those two factors fall out of balance, they risk losing riders or drivers. So, they use surge pricing to correct imbalances—raising the price for rides when demand is very high. All of these factors are controlled by algorithms, not people. Uber is also experimenting with driverless vehicles, which will be a new adventure in AI.

E: EXPONENTIAL TECHNOLOGY

Uber exists because of the exponential growth of mobile phones and the diffusion of GPS. These technologies used to cost thousands of dollars and, but now almost everyone has the technology in their pockets.

V: VALUE FACILITATION

Uber's model depends on people, and the value of their company depends on people joining their platform. They need passengers to incentivize drivers, and drivers to meet the needs of passengers. Both sides of the equation find value in meeting each other at specific points and times, and Uber is just the facilitator.

E: ETHICAL CHAMPIONSHIP

Uber has expertly used the first four letters of CLEVER (as well as the last, as we'll see shortly). They understand how to use technology and business models that dominate the 4IR expertly, but when it comes to Ethical Championship, they fell short.

Between 2014-2018, Uber has reportedly lost 20 percent[3] of its valuation—a fact that is counterintuitive, as the business kept growing. They've had a series of ethical scandals[4] and failures related to unfair competition, deception of law enforcement, sexual harassment, and a range of other issues. These scandals have resulted in hundreds of millions of dollars in settlements and the dismissal of the CEO and founder. Despite its brilliant business model, the company has been defined and limited by its unethical blips.

R: RESPONSIVE DECISION MAKING

Uber is brilliant at deploying new solutions and services. It tests them out and uses feedback to determine whether to abandon or carry out ideas on a large scale, a technique that sometimes puts them at odds with more traditional companies. Barclays Bank, for example, wanted to team up with Uber on a credit card, but they had trouble reconciling their time frames for the project. For Barclays, six months was an impossibly short amount of time to implement anything—for Uber, six months was too long. They had to be granted special board approval for the project to run seven months.[5]

3 Theodore Schleifer, "Uber's Valuation Dropped 20 Percent, According to Some Investors," *Vox*, last modified January 11, 2018, https://www.vox.com/2018/1/11/16879370/mutual-funds-uber-wall-street-fidelity-principal-blackrock-valuation.

4 Kate Taylor, "49 Of the Biggest Scandals in Uber's History," *Business Insider*, last modified May 10, 2019, https://www.businessinsider.com/uber-company-scandals-and-controversies-2017-11.

5 Tanaya Macheel, "What Uber Taught Barclays about Agile Development," Tearsheet, last modified December 1, 2017,...

Their risk attitudes were also mismatched. Uber's strategy is to test by rolling out services and then improving as time goes on. Barclays operates in a more heavily regulated industry and is averse to risk. Uber, on the other hand, worries that if they were to design something to 95 percent completion before launching it, they would leave little room for improvement unless they perfectly predicted what was going to happen.

A NEW ERA

Grasping all the aspects of CLEVER, even if you never employ some of them, helps you understand our current economic landscape. It helps you see what's going on outside of your company's and industry's sphere so you can find what opportunities exist.

Making positive changes within your company helps not only the business, but your career as well. By successfully predicting challenges, pitching strategic solutions, and implementing them successfully, you are acting as a leader.

The reasons corporations exist is because they have the resources and can take the risks that individuals cannot chance on their own. From a societal perspective, creating value from limited resources is an ethical thing to do. Although many of us live in an age of wellness and abundance, the truth is we have limited resources as a planet. It's our duty to create value, not destroy it.

...https://tearsheet.co/modern-banking-experience/what-uber-taught-barclays-about-agile-development/.

The 4IR is an era defined by VUCA and is becoming ever more VUCA. Using the CLEVER framework is no longer just useful—it's necessary for survival. I want you to use the CLEVER model to engage with your peers, employees, colleagues, and bosses. I want this understanding of strategic change and response to help you expand your role as a leader. You must be the driver of change. In doing so, you can help others succeed with you.

SHARE YOUR CLEVER MOMENTS

I wrote CLEVER to start a conversation.

My vision is a community of CLEVER business leaders worldwide, inspiring each other, and learning from each other's successes. I am a professor, and I take pride in my job as an educator. My lessons, however, are only useful if they help my students and my clients solve real problems that matter to them. I, too, must embrace CLEVER.

To do so, I need to hear your answers to the questions at the end of each chapter. You can send them to me via email (answers@alelanteri.com). Send as many answers as you want—one or all of them. They can be lengthy and elaborate or brief and intuitive. Your answers will not be graded!

You will help me find the right way to support you and your company, as well as other leaders like you and their companies, to master the 4IR. You will help kickstart a conversation.

The conversation continues with new content, videos, and case studies on www.alelanteri.com.

ABOUT THE AUTHOR

Alessandro Lanteri, PhD is a Professor of Entrepreneurship at Hult International Business School in Dubai and London, and teaches executive education programs at ESCP Europe and Saïd Business School, University of Oxford. Alessandro has advised multinational corporations, the UN, and the World Economic Forum, and worked with startups and family businesses across Europe, the US, the Middle East, Asia, and Africa. His research has been published in *Harvard Business Review* and MIT *Technology Review* outlets, *LSE Business Review*, the *World Economic Forum Agenda*, and *Forbes*. A popular keynote speaker, Alessandro's TEDx talk has been viewed more than 200,000 times. To learn more, visit www.alelanteri.com.

Made in the USA
Columbia, SC
28 November 2019